# Uncle Sam,

# The Monopoly Man

# William C. Wooldridge

ⓞⓞⓞⓞⓞⓞ

# UNCLE SAM,

# THE MONOPOLY MAN

ⓞⓞⓞⓞⓞⓞ

Arlington House
New Rochelle, New York

FIRST PRINTING, OCTOBER 1970
SECOND PRINTING, DECEMBER 1970
THIRD PRINTING, APRIL 1971

Library of Congress Catalog Card Number 74-115351

ISBN 0-87000-100-0

MANUFACTURED IN THE UNITED STATES OF AMERICA

⊙⊙⊙⊙⊙⊙

# Contents

⊙⊙⊙⊙⊙⊙

# Preface

SEVERAL YEARS AGO I WAS A STUDENT AT ST. ANDREWS University in Scotland, and I found that placing a telephone call constituted one of that environment's greatest challenges. Private phones were too expensive to be commonplace, so a prospective telephoner first had to accumulate four pennies for each call he desired to make, a project complicated by the absence of any nearby commercial establishment open beyond the hour of six or seven. Next, the attention of an operator had to be engaged, in itself a sometimes frustrating undertaking, whether because of inadequate manpower or inadequate enthusiasm on the switchboard I never knew. Finally, since the landward side of town apparently boasted no more telephones than the seaward, a long wait frequently followed even a successful connection, while whoever had answered the phone searched out the party for whom the call was intended. A few repetitions of this routine broke my telephone habit altogether, and I joined my fellow students in communicating in person or by message when it was feasible, and not communicating at all when it was not.

Nevertheless, the experience rankled, so I raised the subject one night in the cellar of a former bishop's residence, which now accommodates the student union's beer bar. Why were the telephones socialized? Why weren't they a privately owned utility, since there was so little to lose in the way of service by denationalization?

The reaction was not, as might be expected, in the least defensive, but instead positively condescending. It should be self-evident to even a chauvinistic American that as important a service as the telephone system could not be entrusted to private business. It was inconceivable to operate it for any other than the public interest. Who ever had heard of a private telephone company?

That incredulity slackened only slightly after a sketchy introduction to Mother Bell (then younger and less rheumatic than today), but at least the American company's example demonstrated that socialized telephone service was not an invariable given in the equation of the universe. My friends still considered the private telephone idea theoretically misbegotten and politically preposterous, but no longer could it remain literally inconceivable, for there we all were sitting around a table in the bishop's basement talking about it. It had been done. It might—heaven forfend—be done again. The talk necessarily shifted from possibility to desirability, to what lawyers call the merits of the case.

Similarly, to redirect discussion surrounding a number of government monopolies is the object of this book. Like the St. Andrews students, Americans show a disposition to accept our government's customary functions as necessarily the exclusive province of government; when city hall has always done something, it is difficult to imagine anyone else doing it. I am going to recount a number of instances in which for better or worse someone else *has* done "it," with the hope that these anecdotes will awaken the reader to at least the possibility of choice.

When an activity is being undertaken for the first time, the operation of the Telstar communications satellite, for instance, people keenly feel and sharply debate their option for public or private ownership. Discussion of the costs and advantages of each alternative accompanies the final choice. But once the choice is made and a little time passes, an aura of inevitability envelops the status quo, and consciousness of any alternative seeps away with time.

Today, most Americans probably feel the telegraph naturally belongs within the private sphere, and few doubt the Post Office should naturally be a public monopoly. "Naturally," however, in such a context means only that's-the-way-it's-been-for-as-long-as-we-can-remember, an Americanized version of Pope's declaration that "Whatever is is right." Yet few could think of a convincing *a priori* rationale for distinguishing the postal from the telegraphic mode of communication. At least one Postmaster General could not: in 1845 his Annual Report prophesied intolerable competition from the telegraph and suggested it might appropriately be committed to the government. At that early stage in its history, the telegraph might conceivably have become a government monopoly for the same reasons the Post Office already was, but the mere passage of time has obliterated any consideration of whether they were good reasons or bad reasons.

By reopening some of these cases, I hope this book can stimulate an awareness of the freedom of action the country can enjoy in the selection of methods for accomplishing what are normally considered exclusively governmental responsibilities. In short, I want to expand the conversation at St. Andrews to include courts, roads, schools, the Post Office, and even coinage. This is to be distinguished from a proposal, much less a blueprint, for the denationalization of any given industry. The possibility of choice, not the choice that should be made, supplies the theme. Saying that much will not conceal from any reader the book's animation with a certain sympathy and affection for the entrepreneurs who have from time to time sallied forth to do battle with a governmental monopoly. Nevertheless, recalling and enjoying the story of, say, G. Lindenmuller, coiner extraordinary, is not to be equated with proposing an immediate sale of the United States Mint to private parties, if for no other reason than the booklength treatment that would be required to detail the merits of expanded private participation in any single one of the half-dozen sectors treated here.

The scope of the book enforced these limitations on its depth, and at the same time suggested a lighthearted rather than severely scholastic tribute to the Davids who time and again have taken up the sling out of lust for adventure or gain; readers will find a bibliography at the end but few footnotes along the way. David versus Goliath has always been a good story, and to keep it so, technicalities have been minimized. Always, too, the tale has been meant to be more than a good story. Merely suggesting the possibility of a contest should intrigue a number of people, whether new leftists disillusioned with government bureaucracies, or old rightists immemorially suspicious of the power-hungry state, or simply eternal technocrats curious about more efficient alternatives to government services. Somewhere along the line from Henry Fielding's private police to Christopher Bechtler's private coins to Thomas Murray's private post office to the Urban League's private schools, each should encounter fresh facts and consequently each, on returning to his own immediate concerns, should be

10

able to examine those concerns with a heightened consciousness of alternatives.

Coming to grips with so many different fields has no doubt resulted in errors which a specialist will detect in the chapter covering his area of expertise, but it seemed important to try to bring all this scattered material together in one place. The text will show that the title itself is a misnomer: the monopolies are not all Uncle Sam's, but occur at every level of government, and they are not all absolute monopolies, just responsibilities habitually ascribed to the state.

This florilegium would not have come into being without the assistance of others. A part of Chapter One originally appeared in *Rally,* and the magazine's editor, Timothy J. Wheeler, suggested the theme of the book. The Winchester Foundation sponsored the research on which Chapter Eight is based. My wife Joyce spent many hours culling raw material from newspapers for the chapter on private black schools, and then worked still more on putting it together. Finally, the legal asides represent gratuitous borrowings from a dozen different professors and practitioners with whom I have had the advantage of working over the last several years.

Charlottesville
*January 1970*

ⓞⓞⓞⓞⓞⓞ

# CHAPTER ONE

# The Post Office

If Congress cannot carry the letters of individuals as cheaply as individuals would do it, there is no propriety in their carrying them at
all.

—LYSANDER SPOONER, 1844

THE UNITED STATES POST OFFICE WAS ORGANIZED
in 1789. It went $40.00 in the hole that year, thereby establishing
one of the most venerable of American traditions. More than a
decade before Parson Weems immortalized the cherry tree, the
United States Post Office was losing money. For most of the
years since Postmaster General Thomas Osborne reported the
first deficit to President George Washington, it has continued to
lose money, receiving all the while less critical attention than
the cherry tree it antedates. Yet the stars in their courses do not
ineluctably dictate a government postal monopoly. One of the
most fascinating and least known chapters of American history is the saga of the private individuals who in the nineteenth
century captured between a third and a half of the Post Office's
entire business, forced the government monopoly into a fight
for its very life, and drove some officials to the prediction that
the United States Post Office was doomed to an early collapse.
This point was reached in the 1840's, but the story begins one
hundred thirty years before, when a governmental postal
monopoly was first established on the North American conti-
nent.

In 1692 the King of England granted Thomas Neale a patent
(license) to provide postal service in the American colonies, but
in 1710 the British government itself assumed the sole right to
conduct the business. Rates were increased all along the line to

about twice the previous level. The colonists shortly stopped using the royal service, and the King lost money on his putative monopoly for thirty-five years.

Correspondence did not simply cease when the rates went up. Rather it shifted to an extensive private network of postal riders, who carried the mails in cheerful defiance of the law. Not the least energetic of the extragovernmental posts were conducted by men ostensibly in the King's employ, men not above accepting a private commission on the side, who stuffed His Majesty's mailbags with "bundles of shoes, stockings, canisters, money, or anything they get to carry, which tears the Portmanteaus and rubs the [legal] letters to pieces." So reported Hugh Finley, a Canadian postal inspector sent out by the crown to investigate the anemia afflicting the government service. At Newport, Rhode Island, he found "two post offices, the king's and Peter Mumford's," and everywhere the independent carriers flourished, beyond the power of the King to interdict. Finley reported an indignant public would tar and feather anyone who interfered with its private postal arrangements, and no jury would convict a rider of violating the law, since, as a later historian summarized, the official postal service was a "byword and a hissing" to all concerned.

This silent standoff between King and colonies sixty years before the Revolution foreshadows all the major features of the developments that almost put the United States Post Office out of business in the 1840's. Private carriers offered better service at a lower price than the government. Public sympathy made it impossible for the government to move against them successfully.

Our original postal laws borrowed heavily from the British laws the colonists had so cavalierly ignored for many years, but the service must have markedly improved, for there is very little evidence of any serious private competition with the government until the 1830's. Of course, any such competition would have been illegal, but that obstacle had not inhibited the eighteenth-century carriers.

By 1840, however, something had happened. The country was ebulliently heaving in the early stages of industrialization. Speculation was rife, commerce boomed and plummeted, and the earliest railroads tentatively webbed out from the major cities, a curiosity rather than a threat to the thriving steamboats. Business attained a systematization and volume that demanded something more than casual intercity communication, and the railroads and steamboats made something more possible.

This if ever was the era of real-life Horatio Algers, and one of them realized that the Post Office was not keeping up with transportation progress in general and the demand for efficient communications in particular. His name was William F. Harnden. In 1839 he invested his savings in a half-bushel carpet bag and "without capital, health, or influence" laid the small beginnings of the first American express company.

A set of accidents had transformed Harnden from a lowly clerk to a man who in a few years would be the incubus of the United States Post Office. Frail son of a Boston housepainter, he did not have the physique to follow his father's outdoor trade, and instead found work as a clerk for the Boston and Worcester railroad. But that calling, too, overtaxed his always precarious health, for sixteen hours in a ticket office was as debilitating as twelve hours on a painter's scaffold was exhausting. Casting about for some healthier vocation, Harnden conceived the idea of chaperoning the messages and remittances of Boston businessmen to New York and vice versa.

Harnden hardly began his route in the thought of breaking the Post Office monopoly; instead, he contemplated something akin to a present-day express or armored-car service for packages. In fact, he was well aware of the postal monopoly laws and did not choose to flout them. With his characteristically meticulous attention to detail, he instructed his employees to "receive nothing mailable. You will have no small number of Post Office spies at your heels. They will watch you very close. See that they have trouble for their pains." But, as a postal inspector reported it, the letter-carrying business practically forced itself upon Harnden. Merchants importuned him to give their letters the benefit of his expedition. The devil could be accorded his due if regular United States postage were collected on the letters in addition to Harnden's fee, but the Department eventually hit upon a more reasonable expedient: making the diminutive ex-ticket clerk government contractor for transportation of letters between Boston and New York. In this capacity Harnden is said to have carried twenty thousand dollars worth of legal mail in two and one-half years.

That statistic, one of the few available, gives some idea of
the volume of Harnden's business in the early years, substantial notwithstanding discouragingly thin early returns, sometimes as low as a few dollars a day. Like many of his successors,
Harnden had a keen sense of advertising, and the story is told
of his overhearing a colleague place an order for a thousand
white cards "a little smaller than his hand." "His hand!" Harnden interjected. "Have them a foot square, five thousand of
them and the color red." Such tactics evidently proved emi-
nently successful; the distinction between mail carried on contract for the Post Office and that transported entirely on private
account did not seem to hold up well, and within a year, despite
his disclaimers, Harnden's express had a near monopoly on
commercial mail moving along its route.

A merchant testified that he did not send one letter in fifty
by the regular Post Office. The New York postmaster lamented
that he had lost a third of his revenues to the private express,
and the estimated loss in Massachusetts was forty percent.
Harnden had recruited his brother Adolphus, another minuscule individual—together they weighed under two hundred
pounds—to aid him as the business expanded, and the latter's
death in the burning of the steamer *Lexington* in 1840
confirmed what many had believed. When Adolphus' body
washed ashore, one hundred forty-eight letters were found
with it, all of which he had been carrying out of the mails. The
express had become a private post office.

Harnden, too, died prematurely a few years later at the age
of thirty-three, his frail constitution no more impervious to the
hardships of big business than to those of housepainting. His
business was only five years old, and had he survived and con-
centrated on its domestic side (his last years had been devoted
largely to unprofitable international operations), Harnden
would assuredly have grown rich competing with the Post
Office, for his career amply demonstrated that the customers
were there, eager for the opportunity to avoid the government's
service, and the Boston–New York route itself was an extremely lucrative one.

So signal a success in so short a time, overflowing from one
half-bushel carpet bag, attracted competition even within
Harnden's lifetime. Alvin Adams, a Boston produce man who
had been orphaned at the age of eight, started a rival route;

fourteen years later the operation was capitalized at a million dollars. Harnden himself enlisted Henry Wells (later of Wells-Fargo) in Philadelphia in 1840 to take advantage of Wells' acquaintance with the Hudson River steamboat magnate Daniel Drew, a contact that allowed the new partnership to extend its services to Albany. (Until then the riverboat captains had jealously guarded what was fast becoming an extremely profitable sideline by declining to transport other carriers on reasonable terms.) Having reached Albany, Wells dreamed of expresses to all parts of the frontier, a notion at which Harnden scoffed: "Do so if *you* choose to run an express to the Rocky Mountains; *I* choose to run an express where there is business." Wells successfully rose to that challenge and by 1845, having joined forces with W. G. Fargo to form the famous partnership, envisioned routes to Cleveland, Cincinnati, Chicago, and St. Louis for their Western Express.

That far-flung network of routes represented impressive expansion from the days only five years before, when Wells himself, bearing a single sack for his clients' letters and parcels, had caught the train going west from Albany to Buffalo once a week. Every trip was a new adventure, since Buffalo in those days stood on the fringes of what Easterners considered civilization. A quarter-century later Wells recalled his weekly treks with the gusto of a Rocky Mountain trapper. The old capitalist especially remembered the danger to rail passengers posed by the occasional springlike coiling up of the line's strap rails; they tore through the wooden bottoms of the carriages and could maim anyone caught unawares.

There were political problems as well. Like the King's colonial post riders whose extracurricular business Hugh Finley had reported, a government postal carrier tried to persuade Wells to add him to the company's payroll and entrust to him the daily (demand for the service had by then necessitated daily runs) consignment of letters and parcels, since the government carrier's job required that he cover the route anyway. Wells demurred, and when the government carrier did succeed in interesting one of Wells' competitors in the proposition, Wells was able to beat him out of business in a week. It was almost as if the mere ride in a government mailbag alchemically would make a letter late.

Henry Wells also instituted a Philadelphia–New York express. The government rate over this route was twenty-five cents, and Wells' six-cent charge, initiated in 1843, bereft the United States of both business and sympathy in Philadelphia. To the fiery Wells' vast amusement, the government remonstrated and protested. As fast as the United States could arrest his messengers, indignant citizens bailed them out. By this time he had added stamps to his other postal paraphernalia, and sold sheets of twenty for a dollar, giving the volume mailer the further discount of a cent. In a spirit of public service, or private deviltry, Wells offered to carry the government's mail for one-fifth of the government rate, but the offer was summarily rejected. Eventually, however, the United States did have to lower its fee, and Wells (in a retrospective speech before the American Geographic and Statistical Society) took a large part of the credit.

Anyone who could afford the price of a railroad ticket could become an illegal postman. For a very few years the East Coast enjoyed something that has never since recurred: a private, competitive postal service with constantly decreasing rates and constantly increasing efficiency, as well as all the normal accoutrements of a mail system. The House Committee on Post Office and Post Roads summarized the development with alarm: "This illicit business has been some time struggling through its incipient stages, but it was not until the year commencing first July 1840 that it appears to have made a serious impression upon the revenues of the department. It has now assumed a bold and determined front, and dropped its disguises; opened offices for the reception of letters, and advertised the terms on which they will be dispatched out of the mails." In short, the carriers had developed the organizational details of a major industry, and together constituted a complete alternative postal system, to which more and more people habitually entrusted their letters, leaving the official service to wither away like the ideal Marxian state.

The business attracted some odd sorts. Alvin F. Harlow, historian of the California carriers to be discussed in a few pages, describes a man named Ross who ran the Worcester-Providence express. He was four feet ten inches tall, sported a black swallowtail coat, crimson velvet collar, plaid trousers, and "sharp toed, upcurving boots." None of the Post Office blue for him; Ross meant his customers' mail to be carried in style!

The prime example, however, of an eccentric converted into a useful human being by the lure of the new industry must be Lysander Spooner. He had been a deistical bachelor who whiled away the hours in the Boston Athenaeum before the success of his American Letter Mail Company earned the fulminations of the Postmaster General. Mr. Wickliffe denounced the "low conniving" that could make enough money during the course of one trial to pay every penalty for ignoring the law. Spooner replied by returning to the shadows of the Athenaeum and shortly emerging with *The Unconstitutionality of the Laws of Congress Prohibiting Private Mails,* a fire-breathing pamphlet from which the epigraph is taken. One can imagine Spooner enjoyed composing his little treatise as much as he did carrying letters.

"If the public are satisfied with the correctness of the principle," Spooner began, "the Company [the American Letter Mail Company] ask their patronage to enable them to sustain it." A postal monopoly, he argued, is derived from the practice of arbitrary governments. "It has no adaptation to facilitate anything but the operations of tyranny." Therefore he dismissed it as inconceivable on American soil.

Spooner analogized the postal power to the coining power; just as any man can stamp and sell his own coins, any man can carry letters. He cited the private minting activities of Christopher Bechtler (whose career is elaborated in Chapter Three) in North Carolina to exemplify the analogy. Today, at least, that particular line of argument will not persuade many people, since a man can be put in jail as quickly for selling his own coins as for selling his own stamps. Yet Lysander Spooner also presented arguments that still merit serious consideration. The Articles of Confederation had given Congress "the sole power" to establish post offices and post roads, while the Constitution conspicuously changed this to "the power," implying by the alteration that it was not an exclusive power. If the question remained open today, it would at least be debatable; but even when Spooner wrote, the practice of many years argued against him.

Switching to arguments of expedience rather than pure legality, Spooner reasoned that if the justification for suppressing private carriers was to protect the revenues of the Post Office, it would be better simply to appropriate to it the deficiency entailed by permitting private competition and allow the people to continue to enjoy the lower rates and faster service of the carriers. And in reply to an old, familiar, and still current argument for the postal monopoly, he stated outright that it was "palpably unjust and tyrannical" for the populous sections of the country to have to support government mail delivery on the frontiers through the payment of high rates on the seaboard. But the real reason the Post Office loathed competition and always fell before it, he concluded, was that "government functionaries, secure in the enjoyment of warm nests, large salaries, official honors and power, and presidential smiles, feel few quickening impulses to labor," a situation that inevitably renders the government postal service "cumbrous, clumsy, expensive, and dilatory." One hundred twenty-five years later a study of the American Economic Foundation reached nearly identical conclusions without quite such fervid prose in an evaluation of Post Office parcel post service. There is a timelessness to bureaucracy that makes the study of its past as instructive as the analysis of its present. "Quickening impulses to labor" understandably do not stir individuals who are responsible to the people they serve only through the dampening medium of the legislature, and therefore these individuals have nothing immediately to gain by pleasing their clientele.

Lysander Spooner's constitutional arguments probably attracted few readers and made fewer converts, but the better service he and the other carriers rendered provided all the persuasion that was necessary. The local presses hailed them because the expresses brought them news from other cities well ahead of the Post Office. Businessmen desperately needed the faster and safer communications provided by the carriers and backed them unswervingly, the merchants of Rochester going so far as to offer Pomeroy's Express, with which Henry Wells had become associated, a subvention of six thousand dollars to begin an illegal daily express. And the public at large accepted the carriers as an indispensable contribution to the speed and economy of their everyday correspondence, seeing no reason to jail a man simply because he ran circles around the Post Office.

The private carriers became, in fact, minor folk heroes, Robin Hoods whose speed and stealth constantly eluded the bungling Postmaster of Nottingham, poachers in a preserve which royal fiat had unpopularly declared its sole domain. Old expressmen romantically recalled full-tilt, cross-country cowboy-and-Indian chases; the spectacle of a carrier's desperate attempt to speed himself and his contraband letters beyond the reach of a government agent must have aroused a natural sympathy for the pursued. A nineteenth-century engraving from *Harpers New Monthly Magazine* catches the tableau: a pack of letters strapped papoose-like to his back, the dashing express agent with horse flattened out in a full run flamboyantly waves his hat to the admiring local farmers, while a small bulldog, later to become an express company symbol, barks at the excitement and two pursuing government agents whip their horses over the horizon. Shades of Paul Revere, Jack Jouett, and Odysseus! Small wonder the people overwhelmingly supported those who scorned the monopoly.

Sometimes the government agents would take their quarry, but when that happened "citizens stood ready with bail-bonds filled out and executed" so the carriers would immediately be released. Judicial proceedings accomplished no more; there were many trials and all of them were futile. One William C. Gray set the standard in 1839. He was accused of carrying letters on the "Lowell [Massachusetts] cars." While the judge learnedly approved the constitutionality and applicability of the postal monopoly law, the jury simply found that Gray had not carried the letters.

A widespread but seldom recorded conviction that the Post Office was bilking the populace explains this surprisingly lawless contempt for the monopoly. Aside from Spooner, the thoughts of only one individual who set down his negative reaction at any length have been found, and they are given here as a specimen of what obviously was a national mood in the 1840's, although this example dates from the years after the Civil War.

Wells-Fargo Express operations in the West, Albert D. Richardson wrote, "illustrate the superiority of private enterprise. Whenever the messengers run on the very steamer, or the same railway carriage, with those of the United States mail, three-fourths of the businessmen entrust them with their letters, which are invariably delivered in advance of government consignments. . . ."

Henry Wells had begun that tradition years before on the

Albany run, giving service almost laughably superior to the government carrier, although they both of necessity rode the same railroad, and no doubt often in the same car.

"The uniform charge," noted Richardson,

for delivering letters is 12 1/2 cents. The company carries them only in stamped envelopes, thus paying a government tax of three cents on every half ounce. Yet the Post Office Department constantly endeavors to suppress it. . . .

When the operations of the Wells-Fargo Company were confined to the Pacific Coast and the steamer between San Francisco and New York, it transported 2.3 million letters annually. Two and a quarter millions of writers paid 9½ cents not to have their letters pass through the Circumlocution Office.

What stronger proof of the folly of government conveying letters? It might with as much propriety sell groceries, convey heavy freights, or deliver washing.

Abolish the Post Office Department. Leave this like the other carrying trades open to private competition, and the mail service of the United States would be performed 50 percent cheaper and 100 percent better than it is today.

The annual lamentations of the Postmaster General in his report to the President, and the few available court records provide additional evidence that Richardson wrote what thousands felt. It is clear that outmaneuvering the Post Office became practically a national sport, carried on in the spirit of Sarge mortifying Lieutenant Fuzz. Every hotel in New England, reported the First Assistant Postmaster General, was a *de facto* post office, and he quoted the Philadelphia postmaster's unhappy prediction that if the private expresses "be not put down, they will ere long put down the Post Office Department."

This was literally true. The *Boston Pathfinder* at one point carried a list of 240 different expresses with connections in that city; postal revenues there fell $8,000 in one year, and over the whole country $200,000 less was earned in 1844 than in 1843. Most revealing of all are the figures of letters carried: it was estimated that private companies carried 15,500,000 of the 42,-500,000 letters transported in 1845, well over a third of the total volume, starting from nothing only six years before. When one notes that they operated for the most part between the major northeastern cities and consequently must have carried a much larger percentage of the mail along the Eastern corridor to attain the nationwide percentages just cited, it becomes apparent that the Post Office was well on its way to becoming a dead letter in that area.

Naturally the Post Office objected. A campaign of prosecutions abruptly ended in 1844, when the courts found that the old legislative prohibition of horse and foot posts could not be read to illegalize carrying mail on railroads. It seemed that only new legislation could ward off the financial collapse of the Department.

With a realistic appreciation of the underlying difficulties, the Senate Post Office Committee brought in a bill that would combine a drastic reduction in postage rates with stiffer restraints on private competition. Even then, however, the bill's sponsor recognized the government's congenital inability to compete successfully with the private expresses; he begged his colleagues "to keep in mind, what he had so repeatedly urged, that it was not by competition but by penal enactment" the private posts were to be destroyed.

It might be asked why Congress fell in so docilely with the Executive's plan to crush the carriers. After all, it was these men's constituents who had bailed out arrested carriers, flatly declined to convict anyone under the postal laws, and made the fortunes of Harnden, Wells and a hundred others.

The reason for Congressional concern as it developed during the debates over the bill lay in a genuine fear for the future of the Post Office. It was the belief of our heartier forebears that the Post Office should pay its own way, and their desire that all parts of the country receive postal service on the same terms. But if the lucrative northeast routes were completely won over by private enterprise, it was contended that the rest of the system could operate only at a greater loss than Congress was willing to bear.

The bill passed, not without protest. Opposition focused on the proposal for lower rates. After all, only "businessmen, merchants, city belles, and lovesick swains" write letters anyway —why should a plantation owner have to subsidize their scribblings through the higher taxes necessitated by lower postal rates? The legislation was stigmatized as a New York bill, and everyone knows of the "parsimonious meanness, grasping avarice, and love of monopoly" of New Yorkers. As these quotations indicate, the votes broke generally along sectional lines, the South seeing low postal rates, like the tariff, as a tax collected from the nation at large solely for the benefit of the commercial classes.

In the face of determined resistance, the specter of Post Office bankruptcy carried the day. "Much the largest proportion of [the nation's] correspondence" was already carried by private hand, the bill's sponsor warned. The Post Office had been rendered "odious" in the eyes of the people. The laws guaranteeing a government postal monopoly were totally inoperative and must remain so for as long as the private carriers could offer a tariff so much below the government's.

The bill passed in 1845, but it did not succeed in wiping out the carriers. Many of the private companies hung on, and a Committee of the House of Representatives actually reported out a bill whose Draconian features might well have made it the final solution desired by its sponsors. The bill, which did not pass, would have allowed summary seizure of a man suspected of carrying contraband letters, levied a fine of $100 a letter, and permitted the carrier's retention in jail until the fine was paid.

A still further reduction in postage, from five cents to three cents, finally enabled the government to regain most of what it had lost in the East. This was the origin of the three-cent rate, which was not exceeded until our own times.

To recapitulate the extraordinary: in five years private competition captured between a third and a half of the American letter-carrying business, drove postage down to one-eighth of its former maximum, and brought the United States Post Office within sight of extinction.

Only in the 1840's was the very existence of the Post Office threatened by the superiority of private service, but independent carriers made history long after that. The Pony Express conjures up pictures of young Bill Cody fleeing a host of bloodthirsty redskins. The saddlebags slung over his mount carried mail in the tradition of Harnden, and legally, too, since there was no government route going west from St. Joseph, Missouri, the Express's jumping-off point; to be doubly safe Russell, Majors and Waddell required that all Pony Express letters be carried in government envelopes. Unlike its predecessors, the Pony Express failed. Ironically, the most famous of all the private posts was one of the least successful.

A United States specialized stamp catalogue lists issues for about one hundred fifty private expresses. It is to philatelists that we owe much of our knowledge of the expresses' local operations; history books have overlooked this particular saga in American communication. While they existed, they pioneered many services the Post Office later adopted, providing a classic example of the small operation that feels compelled to experiment and innovate, with results that ultimately trickle up to the giant after immediately benefitting itself. Somewhere, however, the upward trickle was arrested; *Godey's Ladies Book,* for instance, has never had occasion to compliment Uncle Sam on his five collections and four deliveries daily, as it did Blood's New York Express a century ago.

The final blow fell in 1883. Again companies had sprung up by offering a service the Post Office could not. In large cities, particularly New York, fleets of messengers regularly collected and delivered local mail several times daily. Twenty-three years before, this had been held legal, on the grounds that the messengers did not operate over post roads. Congress, however, closed the loophole. In the determinative case, Elihu Root argued for the government against one Rastus Ransom. Ransom lost, and the Post Office succeeded to the baneful monopoly it still enjoys.

The judges in 1883 were affected by the same consideration that impelled Congress to act in 1845: the "calamitous reduction" in Post Office revenues that would follow any toleration of competition. The unquestioned assumption—that the Post Office cannot successfully compete—is revealing.

In 1845 that assumption was linked to a desire to make surplus revenue from high volume routes pay the losses on low volume routes. By low volume routes, officials meant such trips as the old run to New Orleans, from the major eastern depots across hundreds of miles of sparsely settled hinterland to the Mississippi River port city. The rationale was a product of the American frontier; Lysander Spooner to the contrary, the American people by and large were willing to subsidize mail delivery to those who pushed out beyond the centers of population, and a majority of their representatives felt this could best be accomplished by insuring the Post Office's revenues by guaranteeing its monopoly. A few people, such as Joshua Levitt of the Cheap Postage Society, inveighed against this theory, which in effect demanded that letter writers in New York pay a tax on their every epistle for the benefit of would-be correspondents in Oregon. The protests never struck a responsive chord.

With the demise of the frontier the traditional rationale for the postal monopoly passed away, too, but its ghost has survived in remarkably good health to this day. George Bernard Shaw, no less, revived the theme in *The Intelligent Woman's Guide to Socialism* over forty years ago; private competition could not be allowed because it would skim off the "cream" of the business, leaving the unprofitable (theretofore frontier) routes to the government. The argument persists, and one wonders how elbow-to-elbow the country will have to become before the various permutations of the frontier theory of government postal monopoly are finally laid to rest.

The frontier theory was already a rationalization one hundred thirty years ago; the practical explanation of the postal monopoly skipped from the lips of Major Hobbie, Assistant Postmaster General, when Henry Wells brashly volunteered to take over the government's mail services. "Zounds, sir," Major Hobbie is said to have exclaimed, "it would put sixteen thousand postmasters out of office!" The only implausible aspect to the story is the "zounds"; the motivation for postal monopoly it reveals rings as true today as it presumably did in 1840.

The frontier theory might not have survived so long without reenforcement from a vague feeling that a postal monopoly is "natural." The notion prevails that it costs one firm much less to deliver two letters than it costs two firms to deliver one letter apiece. Commentators conjure up the specter of four postmen from four different companies following each other up the sidewalk to a single house and each handing over a single letter to the occupant, at a cost higher than necessary if all four letters had been entrusted to one man.

A true natural monopoly should also be an inevitable monopoly, for sooner or later competitors will be unable to match the smaller unit costs that accompany increasing size and consequently will have to abandon the business to a giant. A plastic geranium blooms more naturally than a monopoly that requires penal statutes for its protection. Particularly for a government department that starts with ninety-nine percent of the market and therefore enjoys the maximum possible benefit of any economies of scale, profitable competition from private citizens should pose no threat.

Readers need only recall the over two hundred private expresses that at one time served the single city of Boston to conceive serious doubts about whether there is anything natural, or even remotely economical, about entrusting postal service to a monopoly. Not even the putative beneficiary of the monopoly, the frontier, has always appreciated its supposedly favored status. In the years after the California gold rush, the Forty-Niners and their successors found occasion to regret the government's interest in their mail service. What happened in California demonstrates well the feasibility of unlimited postal competition even on the frontier.

An occasional argonaut with less than a Jasonic constitution somehow survived the cross-country trek or long sea voyage and isthmian portage only to find on reaching the coast that his strength was inadequate for the back-breaking work of panning gold out of the California foothills. One such weakling, following in the footsteps of the puny Harnden, exchanged his pickax for a mailbag in June of 1849. Alexander H. Todd, Harlow recounts, travelled through Sonora, Columbia, Mokelumme Hill and many of the other motley overnight mining towns levying the homesick immigrants a dollar a head as the price of inclusion on a list of men for whose mail he would call at San Francisco. The Post Office, the only Post Office, was located in San Francisco, and letters came high when a man had to take several days or a week off from the diggings to check his mailbox on the coast, with no guarantee that a letter would be waiting for him even then. So Todd had no difficulty in signing up enough miners to insure the profitability of his maiden voyage, even if he had had to return without a single letter. On reaching the city, the would-be mailman took the precaution of having himself sworn in as a postal clerk before securing his clients' happily voluminous mail. It had been piling up in the Post Office there for months, and consequently the postmaster was more than happy to unburden himself of the accumulation. Loaded with letters and as many New York newspapers as he could carry, Todd made his way back to the mining fields and proceeded to strike it rich without the necessity of digging and panning. His supply of *New York Herald*s went at eight dollars an issue, and according to some, he exacted an ounce of gold dust, worth fifteen to eighteen dollars, for each delivered letter, in addition to the dollar a name he had already collected. Though the ounce of gold may be hyperbolical, the toll stood at, at least, several dollars a letter, for even with the onset of competition the figure rarely fell below one dollar. Expensive mail service from Alexander H. Todd, however, was an improvement over no mail service at all from the Post Office Department, and the spindly entrepreneur won two thousand customers within a few months. The San Francisco postmaster soon realized the business potential of mail delivery and began to extort twenty-five cents for each letter he handed over to Todd, in an understandable but altogether illegal desire for a piece of the action.

The explanation for the nearly nonexistent postal service the United States offered to the citizens of California is instructive. Congress made a superficially rational and businesslike decision, decreeing that no new post office could be established unless it could realize sufficient revenues from the sale of stamps to support itself; at the prevailing rates, no new location in California met the test. Postal rates were set legislatively, without much regard for the actual state of the market, and then as now rates fell into broad classes of nationwide applicability—there is no way to adjust them to meet the needs and circumstances of particular localities or particular mail users. Unresponsiveness to the varying requirements of users is almost inevitably built into a government monopoly, for the impetus to adaptation must struggle through a Congress properly more interested in other things and simply not equipped to manage a business. These shortcomings were manifested in gold-rush California by a government postal service that refused to expand because it would not and could not charge enough to cover its costs. The scattered miners would have gladly paid ten times the government price for a letter from home, and did pay that much and more to private carriers. The carriers, of course, felt no compunction about charging enough to provide any services for which a demand existed at the necessary price. Thanks to them, isolated miners could enjoy occasional letters from home.

When the Post Office finally did decide to open a second California office, in Sacramento, the service was so poor that it inspired more rather than less demand for private carriers. A newspaper editorialized disgustedly about the Post Office in California: "It's stuck in the mud half the time, and might as well be the other half. No newspapers at San Francisco are sent up from the Bay, and we understand that the postmaster at San Francisco cannot afford to employ clerks. Who will establish an express? And who will not give a dollar for every letter promptly delivered?" The editor's plaintive entreaty found many takers, and soon dozens of expresses were plying up and down the California valleys. According to some, ninety-five percent of the letters delivered in California were carried by private express, a figure so high that the goverment's operation may be practically disregarded, and the state at mid-century stands as an example of an almost completely private, atomistically competitive postal service. Several years later, when the United States finally did open a few additional offices and offer mail delivery at least in the remote vicinity of some of its patrons, the miners nevertheless continued to patronize the private carriers, now out of choice rather than necessity. The Postmaster General in 1853 reported with discouragement to the President: "The habit of relying on the expresses is continued long after the Post Office and the mail route have reached the neighborhood." That habit may best be explained by the presumption that private carriers were either cheaper, faster, or more convenient than the Post Office, perhaps all three, or that Californians' experience with the Post Office left them permanently indisposed to entrust their letters to it despite improvements in service. At least as late as 1881, many citizens still preferred to pay the carriers' tariff in addition to government postage rather than forgo the superior service available privately.

Depending on the authority whose count is accepted, from 546 to 775 separate private expresses carried on their business in California at one time or another, together providing, by the almost unanimous testimony of all who have left reports, better service than the government. The experience of California casts doubt upon the theory that postal service is a natural monopoly. Particular companies dominated certain localities and individual carriers prospered along certain routes, but the state as a whole supported a multitude of postal services.

Consider only Charles P. Kimball. He became a San Francisco institution by his habit of roving the streets singing his service like a fishwife. His major business was collecting locally letters that were bound outward by steamer. San Franciscans affectionately named him the "Noisy Carrier" for his vocal exploits. They did not trust the Post Office to get their mail from their homes to the wharves, and within a few years made Kimball's fortune.

The carriers and companies found it impossible, whether from lack of resources or lack of patronage or intensity of competition, to absorb all their competitors or drive them out of business. Natural disaster, not economic forces, produced the single greatest consolidation: the California office of Adams and Company was wiped out and Wells-Fargo succeeded to the whole freight business. Nor does it appear that duplication of service entailed great waste. One man could carry only a relatively limited cargo of letters and parcels along the poor trails or precipitous rivers, and whenever the volume of correspondence between two points exceeded the capacity of a manageable bag or burro, it consumed few more resources for two competing carriers to divide the business than for one to undertake it all. In short, economies of scale in practice stopped at the top of the mailbag. It is certainly clear that they did not count for enough to enable the government to make its service as popular as that of the private carriers.

About the same time the Postmaster General was complaining about the Californians' persistence in patronizing the private carriers, Adams and Company administered a crowning insult by issuing its own stamps, a move which finally provoked the retaliation that had been within the Post Office's legal power from the beginning. It issued a proclamation announcing that the law required letters carried outside the mails to bear government stamps, thereby initiating an underground war between the Post Office and the carriers which lasted for years, but from which the Post Office ultimately emerged master of the field.

In the beginning stages of this conflict the carriers enjoyed the nearly unanimous support of California newspapers. The loyalty of the press did not rest on a philosophical or economic dislike of the postal monopoly, nor, for that matter, on any particular preconceptions about postal service at all, although the editorials paraded both in good number. The press stood by the carriers because the carriers had become the fastest and most reliable source of news for the papers of California, far surpassing the Post Office, and the industry did not wish to see so helpful a source cut off. The friendly environment had been nourished by the carriers' intense competition with one another to be the first to supply a given paper with the latest news from the East, earning for their trouble not primarily money but the invaluable newspaper leader, "Word from Boston forwarded by Smith's Express has just reached us that . . ." The cultivated reputation for swiftness, frequently alluded to in the news columns, constituted the carriers' best and often their only advertising. The Post Office, by contrast, felt no urge to run races with the competition with the latest dispatches from the East, and consequently began the guerrilla war of the 1850's, with little editorial sympathy for the government.

Listen to the enraged editor of the *Alta California,* whose spleen Harlow discovered in the July 13, 1855, issue. Provoked by a new flurry of postal prosecutions, he sputtered,

The present Post Office system is the most outrageous tyranny ever imposed on a free people. It forbids us from sending letters by such means of conveyance as we may prefer, without paying an odious and onerous tax to the government. . . . The Post Office system, so far as California is concerned, is a humbug and a nuisance. . . . No branch or department of business would be worse served than they are now, were the whole postal system for California to be discontinued. . . . Our business men generally prefer to pay double postage and send their letters by the Expresses, to waiting for the slow coach of Uncle Sam. . . . Private enterprise has got ahead of [the Post Office]; let it go the way of all superannuated things.

All his and his fellow citizens' indignation, however, could not prevail against the monopoly. The century-old wish that the Post Office go the way of all superannuated things remains ungratified, and the nineteenth-century carriers for the most part are forgotten. All that remains the same is the "slow coach of Uncle Sam," but today, once again, a few entrepreneurs are doing something about it.

ⓞⓞⓞⓞⓞⓞ

# CHAPTER TWO

# The Independent Postal System of America

TODAY THERE ARE NO PRIVATE POST OFFICES. AT least, there aren't any that call themselves that, for merely using the name "post office" may violate the statutes surrounding the government's monopoly. Consequently, the Post Office's most intriguing competitor calls itself "Independent Postal System of America," or IPSA. If the title sounds a little grandiose, it is because IPSA harbors vast ambitions: nothing less than nationwide capture of the third class mail market.

In November 1967 Thomas M. Murray, IPSA's sandy-haired founder, was a self-confident, big-thinking Irish hotel executive, a native of County Sligo transported to Oklahoma, where he ran several hotels and motels, and another small hostelry at home for his wife and nine children. One day that month he listened to a friend, Darrell Hinshaw, gripe about the Post Office over coffee. Hinshaw headed a local advertising distribution business, and firmly believed he could deliver such material—circulars, handbills, and the like—more cheaply and efficiently than the Post Office. He had even developed feasibility figures to support his point. Murray looked hard, secluding himself with the data for a week, the story goes, and barely three months later IPSA began delivering third class mail all over Oklahoma City. In those three months Murray persuaded eleven investors to put $50,000 on the line to cover start-up expenses, with an additional $2,000,000 commitment for expansion. He bought twenty Ford vans and decorated them with a suitably audacious emblem: a map of the United States emblazoned I-P-S-A from California to Virginia. He hired carriers, and signed Goodyear Tire and Rubber Company and a local firm as his first clients.

Murray started on a rocky note: only three of his thirty carriers showed up for work, and the Post Office's attitude was equivocal. Nevertheless, emergency replacements carried the mail, vacationing college students eventually filled out the labor force, and in April 1968 Murray counted his first $500 profit. The Post Office's start-up costs lay nearly two hundred years behind it, while Murray must buy his buildings (of precast concrete with Irish green roofs) as he goes along, but in the month Murray made $500, the United States lost about one hundred *million* dollars on its Post Office.

Now the men at IPSA are talking about a multi-million-dollar business covering every city in the country and some outside it. Franchises have been sold throughout the West, at $10,000 per 100,000 people in the area covered. One group of entrepreneurs paid $1,000,000 for rights to half of Canada, and deliveries have begun in Vancouver. Three partners invested $200,000 in a Dallas branch, in the expectation of grossing that much in the first month of operation from contracts with Krogers, Sears, J. C. Penney, and other retail firms. As of March 1969 Murray had received six hundred franchise applications. Three months later IPSA was delivering mail in twenty-eight states and, according to Murray, planning to service "every hamlet in the United States" by 1975. Installation has already begun on an $18 million computer system that will coordinate franchiser activities across the country.

With characteristic flamboyance, Murray is now talking about expansion to the moon. "They laughed when I sat down at the piano. . . ."

IPSA has an almost guaranteed market anywhere it goes because it outperforms the Post Office on every criterion by which one might evaluate a mail service. IPSA is cheaper: it

charges $25 to deliver a thousand pieces of advertising as op-
posed to the $36 exacted by the Post Office for the same amount
of third class mail. Addressing is not necessary, so the advertiser saves another $7 per thousand, making IPSA cost him only
a little more than half of what the Post Office does. (The Post
Office, incidentally, loses money at $36 per thousand—one rea-
son it has left Murray in peace so far.) IPSA is more precise and
reliable; it will guarantee delivery on a particular day of the
week calculated by the mailer to maximize the impact of his
advertising. The Post Office, by contrast, accepts third class
mail only on a deliver-it-when-we-get-around-to-it basis, and
more than one merchant has printed and mailed thousands of
circulars only to find that they were received days after his sale
closed. Finally, IPSA will pick up mail at a client's office or
printing press and cover the exact neighborhood desired on a
regular basis, so advertising need not be wasted on what are,
statistically, poor prospects.

Official postal service by law must fall into one of four
major enumerated classes, each one of which carries a particular rate and is entitled to a particular type of service. It is
legally impossible to contract with the Post Office for more or
less service at a higher or lower rate, so that customers of IPSA
could not obtain the same treatment from the Post Office no
matter how much they were willing to pay for it. Major mail
users have widely differing needs, but regardless of their individual requirements, they are locked into the same four-class
service, because those are the services provided for on the
books and changing the books is no less major an operation
than obtaining any other piece of legislation from Congress:
time-consuming and inefficient at best. Today a mail user must
choose between the same four classes of service available to his
great-grandfather in 1879. The mere antiquity of these oc-
togenarian classes testifies to the difficulty of obtaining legislative action. Large mailers may sometimes not even need all the
incidents of a particular class of service. For instance, they can
often presort first class mail with little difficulty, but the Post
Office cannot allow any lower rate in such situations, no matter
how many man hours the mailer saves the Department. IPSA,
on the other hand, is free to contract for the particular congeries of services a mailer wants. To rework a famous axiom of
Henry Sumner Maine's, the movement from public to private

postal service is a movement from business by bureaucratically established classes to business by voluntary contract. (Maine was, incidentally, talking about the movement from barbarism to civilization.)

Mail users prefer contracts. Singer-Harris, Piggly-Wiggly, Firestone, Bankers Life Insurance, and Western Auto have signed up in Dallas. Their circulars are regularly delivered to the residential areas they select by a corps of postmen expected soon to number a thousand men, each nattily uniformed in blue and gold. Supervisors, one per ten deliverymen, circulate in designated areas and keep the postmen supplied with mail. Murray's carriers average earnings of $90 a week, plus a share of the profits; one-third of them are housewives who add their earnings to the family kitty.

When one of IPSA's postmen approaches a house, his path varies from that of a Post Office deliveryman, for the latter deposits the mail in a box paid for and installed by the resident. Regardless of the sentiments of the householder on the subject, IPSA cannot, according to the regulations, use the mailbox the patron has purchased. So the IPSA postman leaves his mail in a plastic bag attached to the patron's doorknob—the bags cost the franchiser about $7 a thousand, and he realizes perhaps $10 per thousand from advertisements imprinted on them, so the rule against mailbox delivery has been converted into an independent source of profit. Nevertheless, a question remains as to whether the government can really prohibit a man from allowing another man to put pieces of paper in a box paid for and erected by the first man. A suit may eventually supply the answer. Murray at one point threatened to buy everyone in America a second mailbox, but meanwhile IPSA enthusiastically peddles advertising space on its little plastic bags.

IPSA's customers are businessmen because the law does not allow it to carry first class mail, that is, letters as opposed to advertising, and private individuals do not often have occasion to send third class mail, which is the class generally made up of circulars and advertising matter. But private individuals can speculate about what the government's monopoly on letter-carrying is costing them. The United States loses millions of dollars a year on third class mail; Murray carries it at a profit, though he charges only a little more than half the Post Office's price. The United States, however, makes a small profit on first class mail. That means that private companies, if allowed to compete, could undoubtedly carry it at even greater reductions from the government's monopoly prices than the third class savings provided by Murray and IPSA. But the same statutes that put Adams and Spooner out of business are still on the books, so the private letter writer cannot enjoy the economies IPSA gives the business advertising mailer.

The Post Office could still move against Murray or attempt to suppress IPSA if, inspired by his example, it saw a profit potential in third class mail and desired to exploit it without the inconvenience of competition, for the statutory "letter" monopoly could be interpreted to cover advertising as well as correspondence; it has, in fact, already been applied to such non-letter-like material as bills and computer cards. So Murray exists on the sufferance of the Post Office, his best protection being the wild improbability that the Post Office will ever see even the hope of profit in third class mail.

The government has not interfered with Murray, but neither has it shown any interest in learning from his experience. The Irishman claims he volunteered to explain to the House Ways and Means Committee how he could make money where the government lost it, but found no one who wanted to listen. The government's disinterest, however, is not as loftily and stupidly blind as some might assume, for IPSA really has very little to teach the Post Office. The ways in which IPSA has saved money and turned a profit are for the most part simply not available to the Post Office, for very complex reasons that can be summarized by saying that IPSA is a business and the Post Office is a branch of the United States Government.

Consider only the problem of mail classification. A government service has to be available on equal terms to everyone, and in practice the easiest way of guaranteeing this is legislating an understandable uniformity, since it would be extremely difficult to make a multitude of *ad hoc* classifications accessible on comparable terms to all mailers. Hence, the statutes defining the classes of mail serve a legitimate and necessary function for a government department, however economically superior private contracts are as a method of determining the type of service that will be provided.

It may also be altogether appropriate for government employees to have certain rights and prerogatives not normally available in private business; such privileges have grown up in reaction to political interference with their positions, a danger not so immediately felt in industry. Other privileges reflect public employees' ability to deal directly with Congress concerning pay and working conditions, which ability proceeds from the simple and inescapable fact that postal workers are employees of the government rather than of private industry. In short, the Post Office could study IPSA until familiar with every detail of the operation and still learn little that had any immediate application to its own problems.

IPSA is the most ambitious and largest-scale competitor of the Post Office, but other companies are also chipping away around the edge of the government's monopoly. The American Postal Corporation operates a similar service in Southern California. A number of thriving businesses have grown up carrying mail for corporations and individuals to and from the Post Office. A businessman can wait for the Post Office to pick up its mail and save the cost of company-to-post-office transportation, which is covered by the price of stamps. But where speed has any importance, businesses may prefer to pay for delivery twice rather than to wait for a Post Office pick-up van. The Post Office, of course, has nothing to lose; its burden is lightened by the pick-up and delivery companies that perform services the Post Office would otherwise have to provide. Therefore, a special statute allows this form of private mail, so long as it bears regular postage stamps. Twenty-five years ago one M. J. Santulli took advantage of the exemption by buying a truck and a few mailbags; today M. J. Santulli Mail Service of New York carries thirty million letters a day back and forth to the Post Office for organizations that would rather pay than wait, including St. Francis of Assisi Church and the New York City Department of Welfare. Santulli has over eighty trucks engaged twenty-four hours a day carrying mail. Competitor David Mitchell, owner of Dumor Mail Pick-Up Service, Inc., emphasizes a further advantage: "When companies have their mail delivered by the Post Office Department, they have to accept it according to the Post Office schedule. When they hire us, they tell us what time they want their mail and they make their own schedules." Some years ago the Post Office cut back from three or four business-district deliveries a day to the present two; entrepreneurs have been quick to throw their companies into the breach.

Since the government's monopoly is confined to "letters," parcels can be carried by anyone who wants to do so. One company that has entered the package-carrying business is United Parcel Service. The National Federation of Independent Business in 1968 evaluated the service UPS provided on the West Coast. The Post Office, while paying no taxes, barely breaks even and perhaps even loses money on its parcel business; the system of accounting now in use makes it difficult to say precisely. United Parcel, on the other hand, operates on the same terms as any other business, paying taxes and making a profit as a condition of its continued existence. To send a five-pound package from San Francisco to Seattle by United Parcel costs seventy-four cents and takes, on the average, two days. For the same job the Post Office charges thirty percent more (ninety-five cents) and consumes at least a week and sometimes ten days. If the customer prefers air mail, the price differential becomes even more marked: $1.09 by United Parcel versus $3.02 by the Post Office.

Anyone with even meager experience with Post Office parcel post service will realize that United Parcel need not rely entirely on lower prices to attract the business, for one who mails a package is interested not only in how much it costs and how fast it travels, but also in whether and in what condition it reaches the destination. The Post Office, whatever else it may lack in the way of automated equipment, has devised a means of crushing and mangling even the toughest packages, and developed other, more sensitive machines to destroy the contents of a package without actually breaking it open—the rubber hose treatment. United Parcel tries to do better by its customers, and by repute has succeeded.

Even under present laws, competition with the Post Office in the future can be expected to take ever more imaginative forms. No one thinks IPSA is going to be content staying with commercial mail indefinitely; it is already exploring the possibilities of magazine and newspaper distribution. At least one company, Stewart-Warner, is, in effect, marketing a service for instant transmission of letters and other first class mail. Under the trade name of "Datafax Transceiver," the company sells equipment that transmits letters over telephone cables and reconstitutes them at their destination. Stewart-Warner appropriately calls its product the "Electronic Mailbox," and if communications technology advances at the same galloping pace for the next thirty years that it has for the last thirty, the four-and-one-half-minute transmission time advertised by Stewart-Warner may become commonplace for nearly all letters.

The Post Office itself is experimenting with a variant of the electronic transmission idea, which should calm skeptics who fear that it is farfetched or overly visionary, since the Department has always nourished a peasant distrust of innovation. The Post Office and Western Union plan to telegram letters to distant localities, where they will be delivered in normal course by regular postmen. In 1970, residents of fifteen major cities could send telegram letters by nine o'clock in the evening that would be delivered anywhere in the United States the next day. Western Union is supplying the equipment and paying the costs of this preliminary experimentation, and the plan does not envisage initial electronic copying of written material, but rather a process more akin to sending a conventional telegram. Nevertheless, it augurs well for the future of electronic first class mail, a field in which the Post Office may at present have no statutory protection for its monopoly. Technology could provide a vehicle for circumventing the law, just as it did at the beginning of the heyday of the private carriers, when the railroad introduced a means for carrying letters previously undreamed of and therefore not legislatively preempted.

If electronic communication ultimately makes obsolete the government's nearly two-hundred-year-old monopoly, the ghost of at least one man will have the pleasure of saying "I told you so." In his 1845 Annual Report, the Postmaster General of the United States under President Polk pointed out the disastrous impact the telegraph might have on postal revenues, and suggested that it be nationalized in order to protect the Department's monopoly position.

The prescient Postmaster's advice went unheeded, but it is not inconceivable that he may yet be vindicated if enterprises such as Stewart-Warner's ever have a serious impact on postal revenues, for the Department assiduously guards its prerogatives, and Congress has historically proved willing to fashion whatever new tools it needs to suppress any form of competition. Back in 1895, Post Office lawyers advised an inquirer that the use of pneumatic tubes to convey letters from one person to another could subject him to criminal penalties for violation of the "Private Express Statutes," the set of laws that finally squelched the postal entrepreneurs of the 1840's. If the monopoly extends to underground tubes, someone could think of an argument for including overhead wires as well.

On other fronts, too, the Post Office has moved to preserve the integrity of the law and the monopoly. The variety and frequency of the incidents that have elicited an official response show just how and where the monopoly has chafed worst, and at the same time represent a continuation of the nineteenth-century tradition of spontaneous self-service by postal patrons provoked beyond toleration by the government's tortoise trot or tempted beyond bearing by the savings that come with private arrangements.

A messenger may develop a thriving business in a large office building by holding himself ready to transmit correspondence, reports, and other business papers whenever desired, but the Post Office ruled that out half a century ago, on the at least debatable premise that building corridors constituted "post roads." (The government's monopoly is limited to post roads, that is, all roads over which the government carries mail.) By the letter of the law, a man who wants to send a note across the hall must either carry it himself, entrust it to an employee of his organization, or take his chances with the Post Office; a private carrier cannot legally do the job for him.

If the office across the hall happens to belong to a branch of his own company, the alternatives for communicating with it will, theoretically, still be the same. Nothing in the law permits a corporation to hire private carriers to deliver mail between its own offices.

It cost CF&I Steel Company $2,000 to master this particular wrinkle of the postal laws. With one office in Denver and another in Pueblo, Colorado, CF&I needed rapid mail communications between them. That the Post Office did not supply; to traverse the one hundred twenty intervening miles, it sometimes required the heat of one day and the gloom of two nights. CF&I hired an armored-car service for the job instead, which could, of course, make the trip in a few hours, and which presented the additional advantage of being cheaper than the government. Such inside-the-company mail service (when not actually provided by a regular company employee) is just as illegal as hanging out a private post office shingle and carrying mail for all comers. Perhaps chagrined by the reflection on its own capabilities or motivated by a desire to enforce the monopoly laws that were being flouted, the Denver Post Office quickly moved in on CF&I and persuaded it to drop its armored-car service. At the "suggestion" of the Post Office, the steel company also contributed $2,000 to the government in reparation for the stampless mail it had been sending.

CF&I is not positively compelled to go back to the old two-day service. If it is willing to pay full first class postage on every letter going between Denver and Pueblo, it is free to hire whomever it wants to carry them. This, however, puts the economies of private mail delivery in a very different light; few people wish to pay twice for something from which they hardly get their money's worth the first time. But if the service degenerates completely beyond the limits of acceptability, that may be the only way out. The Public Service Company of Colorado, which paid a bus company to carry its mail for over two years before the Post Office stumbled on the nefarious scheme and halted it, now subsidizes the Department at the rate of nine thousand dollars a year rather than suffer its inadequate service. Apparently in fear of a hike in the Danegeld, the company speaks diplomatically of its arrangements: "Let's just say that the busses have a schedule that more closely parallels our needs."

In the first five months of 1967 the Post Office investigated sixty-seven persons suspected of chiseling away somewhere around the edge of the monopoly. Mighty AT&T has aroused suspicion by utilizing nongovernmental means to transfer the records of long distance phone calls from the place where they are made to the place from which they are billed. Whether such records fall within the scope of the monopoly depends on whether they are "letters," a question whose resolution men like Thomas M. Murray of IPSA must await with more than merely intellectual curiosity, though the metaphysics of the issue would delight a Bradwardine. The question turns on the communication of "live" information, and the determination of just when a datum dies has proved very perplexing. A legal scholar recently applied himself in all seriousness to the problem of whether under the Department's definition a message saying that Caesar was assassinated in 44 B.C. would be a letter. (Answer: yes, if in a personal communication.) If billing information such as that shipped privately by AT&T turns out to be dead in the eyes of the Post Office, bills themselves may not be "live," an eventuality devoutly wished by IPSA, since local bill delivery is one of its most profitable potential markets. It is too soon, however, for Murray to start projecting the additional revenue, for the Post Office several years ago suppressed a three-cent bill delivery service initiated by one J. F. Cokey in Richmond, Virginia, and there is no reason to believe it has had a change of heart on the subject.

The Department's enthusiasm for enforcement may in the future prove its undoing, for if very many AT&T's have huge unnecessary expenses foisted on them by official insistence on the monopoly's prerogatives, they will turn against it politically with more ire than the Post Office has had to face since the days of Lysander Spooner; and a monopoly that is political in origin is always subject to a political demise. It is reported that A&P in the 1930's paid ninety thousand dollars in reparations to the Department for moving various items outside the mails; a few such settlements ought to provide the incentive for a determined legislative attack.

An individual citizen, who on every letter he mails pays a monopoly tax of perhaps two or three cents over and above what he might pay for the same service from private competitors, tends not even to think about the price except when it has recently been raised; though he may silently curse the Post Office's creeping pace, certainly he rarely considers or demands disestablishment. Corporations, on the other hand, face the same loss of two cents here and three cents there on hundreds of thousands of items. The inescapable and expensive realities of the multiplication table have stimulated a less fatalistic approach to the problem of postal monopoly. Sooner or later legislation will be pressed that, as a start, will allow businesses to utilize any means they desire to transport letters and other material among the components of their own organization. So sweetly reasonable a proposal might gain Congressional approval, and perhaps then other citizens would demand selective relief from the monopoly, ultimately leaving it riddled and toothless if not actually toppled. Legislation sent to Congress in 1968 called for a thorough study of the necessity of private express statutes; future historians may mark that date as the beginning of the history of the legalization of free market postal service.

Ordinary citizens will eventually be moved to protest not primarily because of continually increasing first class rates, but chiefly because of ever poorer first class service. Metropolitan newspapers' "Letters to the Editor" columns receive a steady stream of complaining mail, and the writers sound genuinely unhappy. The Post Office should know; in a snafu several years ago, it mailed out thousands of cards announcing National Zip Code Week, only to discover that many of them arrived days after the close of the celebration. Merchants who experience the same frustration with direct mail advertisements for their sales can be very bitter; their customers, too, see little humor in being cordially invited to take advantage of bargains in a sale that ended day before yesterday. A newspaper columnist recounted how he received an air mail postcard and paid the two cents postage due only to discover that it had been mailed three and one-half months ago from a city six hundred miles away; in the meantime, the Post Office had raised the price from six cents to eight. Robert Sherrill once calculated that according to the Post Office's own timetables a letter mailed in Washington at 7:15 P.M. on a Monday evening will not be delivered in New York until the following Wednesday morning—the Post Office, when all goes well, swiftly accomplishing that appointed round at an average speed of five miles an hour. *Time* claims that one month in 1968 all the Social Security checks for Puerto Rico were sent to Honolulu. Within a year, 600,000 citizens have taken the trouble to complain to the Post Office about the service, and if as many had written to their Congressmen, the monopoly might already be besieged.

It is useless to multiply examples of what everybody knows

from his own personal experience: mail service is miserable. The point is that although Americans, as Jefferson said, have always been more disposed to suffer evil while evil is sufferable than to alter the arrangements to which they are accustomed, the evil of the postal monopoly must assuredly be approaching the point of insufferability; so a consideration of the alternatives to socialized postal service is a question of more than theoretical interest. In the next few years Congress is going to be called upon to do something—several bills are pending as this is written—and an understanding of the causes of the omnipresent difficulties of the Department is necessary to decide on the best way out of the mire. Unfortunately, most people think in terms of reforming the Post Office rather than allowing private individuals to compete with it.

Public discontent with present mail service has recently focused a good deal of attention on the postal monopoly, and has led to the best and most detailed analysis now available of the circumstances that hamper the rational and efficient operation of any government business. A former Postmaster General, Lawrence F. O'Brien, shortly after taking office concluded that the Post Office was "one of the most screwed-up things he had ever seen" and provided the impetus that led to the appointment of a Presidential Commission by Lyndon Johnson in April 1967 to investigate the whole Post Office problem. Frederick R. Kappel, retired chairman of the Board of Directors of American Telephone and Telegraph, chaired the Commission, which supplemented its own investigations with reports from outside consulting firms, such as Arthur D. Little, Incorporated, of Cambridge, Massachusetts.

The report of the Kappel Commission analyzes in detail why the Post Office does not work well, and cannot work well as long as it remains a department in the executive branch of the United States Government. It is well worth examining here, for the difficulties the Commission spotlighted in the Post Office are common to any government monopoly, and explain how organizations like the Independent Postal System of America can make money by doing the same thing the government loses money doing, and by doing it better to boot.

"Postal catastrophe"—the total breakdown of the Department in one or more geographic areas—is the Damoclean threat the Commission suspends over the country unless changes are made, and it gives a vivid example. In October 1966 the world's largest postal installation, the Chicago General Post Office, drowned under a tidal wave of ten million letters. Like the villain in Frank Norris's *The Octopus,* poetically brought to justice by burial in the rivers of grain whose transportation he had monopolized, the Post Office was inundated with millions of pieces of mail, which turned an initial minor accident, conveyor belt and elevator failures, into a postal tragedy. As the mail continued to mount, the morass spread from the building into the surrounding streets, where the steady stream of railroad cars and mail trucks snarled traffic for blocks around. It took three weeks to get mail moving out of the office again, and months before the Post Office completely restored normal service, that is, inadequate mail movement as opposed to no mail movement at all. What a former chairman of the House Postal Appropriations Subcommittee summed up as the phenomenon of "no control" was graphically demonstrated in Chicago; like the sorcerer's apprentice, awash in the tide he had called into being, the Department is nearly powerless to govern its minions.

If the problem were merely "no control," the solution would be simply to reorganize the Post Office along more businesslike lines, to rationalize the monopoly rather than abolish it. But the Kappel Commission (without endorsing the idea of competition for the Post Office) carefully pointed out why more internal reforms could not help greatly. In a sentence, a government monopoly means that key business decisions—setting wages and rates, approving postal facilities, and attending to a host of other details—are made by the legislative process, and the legislative process should and does incorporate elements that "do not necessarily bring about what is best for the postal system and its customers."

Take, for example, the simple, everyday question of building a new post office, or the somewhat more complicated issue of whether and when to install expensive mechanization equipment. If the Independent Postal System of America were making such a decision, a committee made up of people from the financing, engineering, and operation divisions would formulate a recommendation for the Board of Directors, which would normally accept it as a matter of course, and the contracts would be let. In the Post Office, on the other hand, a diagram of the decision-making process looks like the Snopes Family Tree, involving twenty-two discrete steps and twenty-seven different loci of authority—individuals, committees, divisions, etc. The diagram reproduced below does not represent the ulti-mate possible florescence of a government bureaucracy; that, perhaps, has been achieved in Italy, where a serious count re-vealed that not twenty-two but 3,166 steps were necessary to construct a public school. The Post Office may pale by compari-son, but the Byzantine complexity of its decision process still parasitically saps the vitality from proposals for innovation.

Once a decision is made, up to ten years and usually over five may pass before it can be implemented, for the funds for the facility must be wrung from a reluctant Congress. If the Independent Postal System of America were considering re-placing an obsolete building or purchasing an automation sys-tem for one of its offices, the normal procedure would be to calculate a rate of return on its investment, and if that return were significantly higher than the cost of the necessary capital, to proceed with the outlay. Congressional appropriations, how-ever, are not granted on the basis of an accountant's cash-flow predictions. They depend on political variables totally un-related to whether a facility returns five percent or fifty per-cent on the capital put into it. In the perennial pressure to trim the budget, capital outlays have always been and always will be the prime victims of the scalpel, for the Post Office (or any other government department), it is assumed, can always limp along one more year with a building it has already limped with for two decades of "one more year," and future savings count for little with a Congress obsessed with the present budget. The appropriations process is a many-Indianed gauntlet, which must be run at least twice for every facility. First, the Bureau of the Budget, the President, the House and Senate subcommit-tees, full committees, conference committees, and full cham-bers must pass on the appropriation for site acquisition; there is a theoretical possibility that at any step the appropriation could be dispatched with a quiet blow. Then the entire process starts all over with consideration of the actual building costs.

Even once the appropriation bills have been signed, the

## MOVEMENT OF A MAJOR FACILITY
## DECISION THROUGH THE ORGANIZATION

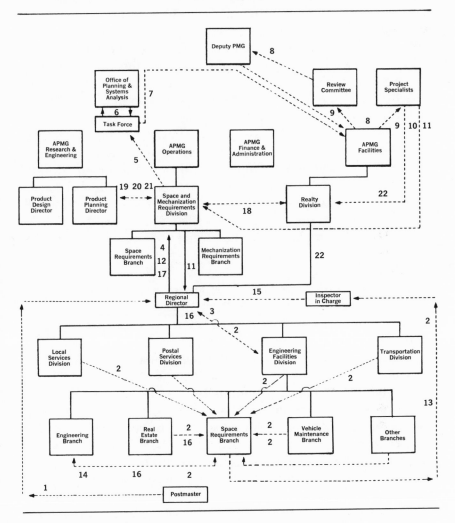

—— Organizational Lines

– – – Movement of the decision

Numbers 1 through 22 represent steps in the decision process.

Source: Arthur D. Little, Inc. Details in Volume 3 of Annex, pp. 3.23-3.34.

From TOWARDS POSTAL EXCELLENCE: THE REPORT OF THE
PRESIDENT'S COMMISSION ON POSTAL ORGANIZATION, p. 44.

From *Towards Postal Excellence: The Report of The President's
Commission on Postal Organization*, p. 44.

planned new postal facility cannot count on uninterrupted progress. At any time presidentially ordered "freezes" on spending can postpone it and every other delayable capital project throughout the government. President Nixon imposed such a freeze in 1969; certain exceptions were made, but not for post offices, desperately as they need modernization.

An observer would be surprised to find that anything ever was built under such circumstances, and in point of fact, large post offices rarely are. The complexities of the procedure make the long trail so nearly impassable that the Post Office may not even bother with it; instead, it resorts to leasing new buildings. The Kappel Commission reported that of sixty-seven major facilities built in the last thirteen years, sixty were leased. Leasing is widely considered to be a more expensive method of financing capital improvements in the long run, but the political imperatives make any consideration of expense almost irrelevant.

The financing dilemma faced by the Post Office demonstrates how shortsighted is the criticism that disassociates the Post Office's failures from the Post Office's status as a government monopoly. The government appropriations process can hardly be other than it is if the country is to remain a democracy; it is the people's taxes that are being spent and their expenditure is appropriately and necessarily hedged about with elaborate procedural complexities designed to prevent unauthorized forays into the Treasury's till. Several centuries, even several millennia, of sad experience lie behind the conviction that too much care cannot be exercised to safeguard the public revenues. It is for the best of reasons that a government employee cannot draw on the Treasury whenever he proposes to make an investment that will return substantially more than the prevailing rate of interest. In a word, government cannot adopt businesslike procedures because it is not a business; the Kappel Commission put it well when it pointed out that the Post Office is "subject to the many checks and balances appropriate to formulating public policy, but completely inappropriate for managing a major economic activity."

The consequences of exclusive public operation of the Post Office, moreover, extend to far more than merely questions of finance. Employees move along in the lockstep of civil service, paid according to their grade rather than their productivity, promoted when a vacancy occurs in the next higher grade rather than when management needs them, and poorly motivated because they know that performance has no necessary correlation with advancement. It could hardly occur to the average postal worker to suggest possibilities for improvement in mail-handling procedures when he knows, first, that there is no way the system can reward him for the idea, and second, that there is rarely any way for the system even to implement the idea, since his local postmaster has virtually no flexibility in managing his branch.

Management, in fact, ultimately rests with Congress, which is merely another way of restating the truism that the legislature is in charge of governing the country, and Congress will have to continue to manage the Post Office as long as it remains part of the government. "Management by legislature," the Kappel Commission nicknamed this phenomenon, and found its quintessence in an amazing volume called the *Postal Manual.* The *Postal Manual* spells out in mind-hobbling detail the pettiest minutiae of postal management; parts of it were written thirty years ago, when management lived in an entirely different world than it does today, and have changed little since then. The *Postal Manual* is the Post Office's own internal law. It could be said to outlaw imagination in postal management; new ideas are illegal because the *Manual* prescribes old ideas. The consequences for efficiency can be easily imagined, and it does not take great political acumen to understand why innovation is simply not a word one associates with the Post Office. Again, the basic problem is not some particular inanity of management, not something that could be attacked by, for instance, a thorough modernization of the *Postal Manual.* Not what the *Manual* says, but the fact that it is there hurts the Post Office; nevertheless, the Department has to be run by regulation, like any other governmental agency.

Still another consequence of the operation of the postal system as a branch of the government is the rate structure. If a task force of philosophers and economists were to sit down to devise the most irrational method for setting postal rates they could imagine, they would be hard put to improve upon the present method of periodic Congressional wrestling bouts, with the strongest lobby winning the lowest rate and the ordinary taxpayer, who for the most part mails only first class letters, subsidizing everyone else. The rate structure is, to use a modern word, politicized; it does not bear any necessary relation to what it costs to carry a given piece of mail. This tendency to tax, in effect, one class of users of a publicly provided service for the benefit of another class of users of the same service is common in federally regulated industries, but it is a phenomenon bound to be short-lived in a competitive milieu: someone will always offer the overpriced service, in this case, first class mail, at a more economic rate and not bother with the rest at all. If Congress thinks, for instance, that newspaper mailers ought to be subsidized because of the educational value of widespread newspaper distribution, it is far more sensible to provide such a subsidy out of the general revenues than it is to load it exclusively on the backs of letter mailers, a class with no particular rational or beneficial connection with publishers. The predictable result of this jockeyed rate structure is that the post offices are loaded sometimes to the point of breakdown with money-losing mail precisely because the material is carried at such bargain prices—bargain, that is, compared with the prices paid by other classes; the Independent Postal System of America carries the same material for even less than the Post Office's money-losing rate.

The Kappel Commission, after spending a year to document all of these failures in elaborate and incontrovertible detail, unfortunately recommended as a solution what at best can be only a palliative. It advocated formation of a government corporation to operate the postal service, to which the Commission would entrust almost total autonomy in day-to-day business affairs and even formidable powers of initiation in rate-making. Certain improvements could reasonably be anticipated from this arrangement, particularly in the area of the financing of new buildings and equipment, for the new postal service would be empowered to borrow money on its own account and so would not have to wait at the end of a long line of politically more appealing candidates for scarce Congressional appropriations. But over the long run all the creation of a government corporation can do is interpose an additional administrative barrier between the provision of mail service and

Congress. One step removed, Congress will still have a firm hand on the rudder through such legislation as the Government Corporation Control Act. And of course there is nothing to prevent the passage of a law simply asserting the legislature's prerogative in one sphere or another of the corporation's management. The postal service would remain an enormous and unwieldy nationwide bureaucracy subject to interference at any majority whim of the legislature. Worse still, it would remain a monopoly.

The Kappel Commission recommendations offer no hope of competition; the Post Office would remain a monopoly, a monopoly administered by a corporation instead of a cabinet department. But no degree of administrative finesse can substitute for competition, and the short history of postal competition in the nineteenth century, reenforced by the more recent emergence of IPSA, ought to suggest how much postal service might improve if it were open to all comers.

The gains to be expected from competition would for the most part come on the economic front: efficiency, service, price. But it should not be forgotten that giving any one body exclusive control over an indispensable service poses dangers that go far beyond the ledgerbook of expense. These dangers are heightened when the monopolist is the government and is therefore entitled to use force to defend its prerogatives. The monopoly invariably will be used to nurture the ideological predilections of those who control it: in the case of the Post Office, Congress's predilections. Zechariah Chafee limned the seductive and fatal logic: we will not illiberally suppress an unpalatable cause such as abolition; we will "merely" close the mails to it. That comforting distinction is still bearing progeny, and only the availability of a private alternative to a government service can keep the government service from being manipulated for repressive purposes. For instance, towards the end of the last century Congress decided to use the postal power to suppress lotteries, by banning lottery tickets from the mails. At that time, however, the Post Office still faced a little residual competition from the express companies, so the lotteries were able to stay in business by shifting their patronage to the expresses.

This is intentionally a relatively neutral example; few peo-

ple will be aroused to passion one way or the other by the fate
of the Louisiana Lottery and its best known sponsor, General
Pierre Gustave Toutant Beauregard. Where there are no strong
feelings, legislative cabals can proceed against their constituents' private enemies. And where there *are* strong feelings, the
situation is even worse, for the postal monopoly becomes a
vehicle for the enforcement of Tocqueville's old but still real
tyranny of the majority. Much of the United States censorship
legislation over the years has been effectuated through the government's stranglehold on the mails. People forget that the first
pages of *Ulysses* to see light in this country (in the *Little Review* in 1918) were burned not by private Comstockians but by
the Post Office. Provincial bluenoses might have shut out the
classic locally, but only the monopoly could successfully cast a
nationwide interdict on its circulation in periodical form. (Unlike magazines, books can feasibly be distributed by freight
rather than by mail, so a Post Office ban is not necessarily fatal
in their case.)

It cannot be assumed that *Ulysses'* immolation is history as
ancient and irrelevant as witch-burning. The Department has
not recently enforced its 1928 exclusion from the mails of all
editions of Boccaccio's *Decameron,* but *From Here to Eternity*
was banned in 1955, and a thrust was made at Aristophanes'
*Lysistrata* the same year. However, the objects of majoritarian
opprobrium change with the times, and future targets may well
be productions that are politically rather than literarily offensive. In 1968 the Supreme Court declared unconstitutional a
statute that prohibited the forwarding of Communist propaganda through the mails without the advance permission of the
recipient. The case caused little stir, but the ban illustrates how
easily monopoly power can be used to squelch political expression.

Thomas Murray might not be the kind of Irishman who
would care for *Ulysses,* much less Communist propaganda, but
chances are that under a competitive regime Margaret Ander-
son could easily have found someone to distribute her magazine for her. Taking your money and your mail to another man
is infinitely more economical than taking your case to the Supreme Court, or for that matter before whatever other tribunal
for the redress of grievances Congress chooses to employ (even

assuming the judicial body thinks the way you do). The cost and delay of litigation are rarely worth the favorable result that may or may not hover at the end of a years-long rainbow.

Woodrow Wilson and Postmaster General Burleson used the government's mail monopoly for a private campaign against the dissemination of "dangerous" socialist ideas for as long as they remained in office; it was three years after the end of World War I before a socialist could entrust a pamphlet to the mails without risking imprisonment. Less popular than socialists, today's minorities, radical and other, ought to be leading a compaign for free market postal service. A monopoly puts fatal powers in the hands of every legislative majority. Sooner or later it will try to exercise them. Thomas Murray, however great his success, will never face that temptation.

⊙⊙⊙⊙⊙⊙⊙

# CHAPTER THREE

# Every Man His Own Mintmaster

SEIGNORAGE HAS TWO MEANINGS: THE PROFIT TO BE
realized from making coins, and the sovereign's sole right to
that profit. The very word suggests the antiquity of the state's
prerogative over coinage, and it is probably the best accepted
of all the government's monopolies. Rarely has anyone objected to it on principle, but on the other hand, it has been
ignored surprisingly often in practice. Until a little over a century ago, coins could be struck with impunity in the United
States, for the statutes creating the coinage monopoly were
pieced together bit by bit in the form of amendments to the
counterfeit laws, and excluded the last private change only in
1863. Therefore, "seignorage" in the United States for many
years could accrue to anyone with the imagination to market
his own coins.

Very unradical people have long taken for granted the
preeminence of private demand deposits, promissory notes,
and commercial paper over green, in-the-flesh money. As a
larger and larger part of the population, armed with the ever
more ubiquitous credit card, capitalizes on various substitutes,
government paper money may suffer still further eclipse.

American Express has sovereignly proclaimed the end of an era in advertisements denominating its service "the new money."

Although coins, by contrast, are still considered the state's prerogative, their past offers more color and more surprises than that of commercial paper. Private coins can be successfully circulated only so long as people want them, and people do not want them unless for some reason tokens meet their needs better than "real" money. That situation frequently recurred right up into the 1960's whenever the supply of government coins became too limited to furnish enough small change.

On those occasions, private money has made a surprising and sometimes substantial contribution to the nation's economic life, despite the disposition even of users to regard it as freakish. How it worked in the face of scorn could be explained by conjuring up a desert island in the manner of the speculative economists of the last century, and following the progress of its economy from barter to money. But in America one hardly need theorize, for we have had our own didactic equivalent of a desert island since 1867, when William H. Seward purchased the arctic wilderness of Alaska. The gold rush of 1898 supplied the impetus to population, more traditionally imparted by a sunken ship, and instead of a few clambering mariners, many thousands of sourdoughs descended upon the Klondike. But otherwise Alaska conformed to pattern: government was not much in evidence, government money was almost nonexistent, and barter, generally with gold dust or furs, was of necessity the principal, though mightily inconvenient, vehicle of trade. When Alaska came to that pass, enterprising merchants began to supply the deficiency with their own privately issued coins, not of fishbone or walrus teeth, to be sure, for technology had progressed a long way since the heyday of desert islands, but generally of aluminum (then a rare metal), bearing the name of their issuer's business.

D. Martin, proprietor of the first store in Juneau, issued one-dollar tokens. The Alstrom Trading Company issued its tokens in denominations of twenty dollars, ten dollars, five dollars, one dollar, and fifty cents. Most other concerns favored smaller amounts, particularly twelve and one-half cents, and sometimes six and one-quarter cents, evincing a somewhat anti-Gallic distaste for the neat gradations of decimal currency. Before the story ended, Alaska had to deal with hundreds of different kinds of money.

The Alaska Pool Hall, the Montana Pool Room, and an assortment of other such places issued their own money, while bars, including one appropriately named "The Mint," enthusiastically took up the business. "Rain Check, Good for One Snort," proclaimed the slug of the Timber Bar of Kenai, while the Pioneer Bar of Ketchikan apparently traded on "points," since its money came in ten-point denominations. If the bingles, as they were onomatopoetically christened, provide a reliable guide, several Italians or Italo-Americans made their way to the Yukon, among them one Ghezzi, a J. M. Giovanetti, whose token was "Good for one Loaf of Bread," and J. Anicichi, who gave his patrons the choice of "One Drink or Cigar" when they redeemed his tokens, evidence either of cheap drinks or of noble cigars on the Alaskan frontier.

Abercrombie's of Ketchikan issued two-cent, four-cent, and eight-cent coins redeemable only in lots of two hundred, fifty, and twenty-five respectively. Another token urged its holder to "Take me to Harry and Charley, Cordova House." Only the imagination and business sense of a proprietor governed the denomination, value in kind, or redeemability of a coin, so practically every issue differed from every other in one or more of these particulars. Sugiya and Company, Salmon Packers, for instance, issued ship money in denominations of five dollars and less, which they would honor only on board their vessels.

Some of the pieces struck a Chamber of Commerce note: Chitina, site of the largest copper nugget ever discovered in Alaska, produced copper pieces bearing the legend "Native copper from Chitina," while a different locality advertised "From the land of gold, where there is plenty for all." Perhaps one can detect a certain amount of humorous boosterism in the coin inscribed "W. Jensen, at the Louvre call for Slemp's beer"; Jensen's saloon, however well supplied with Slemp's or even barroom art, could not have arrogated the name of the museum with a straight face. Some of the later tokens were in fact issued by Chambers of Commerce or benevolent societies with inscriptions urging that the holder save them for a souvenir rather than spend them, advice worthy of some Yukon Necker, since an unredeemed token was money in the pocket of the issuer.

A one-man hole-in-the-wall might produce its own money, such as the twelve-and-one-half-cent piece issued by the Juneau Arctic Barber Shop. A great territorial enterprise might as well; the Northern Commercial Company operated over one hundred stores all over Alaska, so its tokens never travelled far from a source of redemption even if for some reason they should fail to pass in other establishments. Private money even transcended national boundaries; the coins of the North American Trading and Transportation Company were as acceptable in its Canadian stores as its Alaskan, and so become a truly transnational currency.

Everyone familiar with desert islands might guess what happened next. Commerce should have suffered from the number and variety of bingles—what was a token that was good for a cigar in the Moravian mission outpost at Bethel worth in Fairbanks? Certain storekeepers should have realized the potential of pushing as many tokens in change as they possibly could, secure in the belief that few would ever find their way home. Counterfeiters should have applied their skill to reproducing the high denomination pieces. And finally, these multitudinous inconveniences should have cumulatively rendered all such private money worthless and removed it from circulation, reducing Alaska once more to barter or creating a demand for government fractional currency (change).

Seward's peninsular Folly, however, failed to follow that script. Whatever the inhibitions on circulation may have been, they did not grow chronic enough to make the use of bingles impossible. Apparently proprietors found it in their own best interest to issue only what money they needed for convenience' sake, which was little enough, to judge from the prices collectors pay for the surviving tokens. And citizens either devised a way to evaluate the miscellany of pieces, or spent them primarily in the stores of their origin, for bingles continued in use until outlawed in relatively recent times.

A story about their outlawry, although possibly apocryphal, in itself shows what wide acceptance the private money earned. An Alaskan—make him an Eskimo, since the whole affair has an implausible ring—travelled to Seattle, Washington, and in the course of his wanderings decided to communicate his whereabouts to the folks back home. Having entered the Seattle Post Office to purchase the necessary stamps, he was shocked and distressed when the clerk refused to take bingles in payment. Such was the indignation of Alaskans at this slight to their state, the story goes, that their representatives illegalized private money shortly thereafter.

Present-day inquirers may play Frazier and attempt to extract some useful kernels of fact from the myth, or at least with its aid to divine prevailing attitudes. First, bingles had become such an Alaskan fixture that a citizen saw nothing inherently absurd in trying to buy stamps in the United States with them. Second, the use of bingles survived the frontier scarcity of government money which initially inspired them; bingles remained popular with merchants, though hardly essential, into modern times. Third, it took a positive law to remove them from circulation; the natural advantages of official money did not automatically carry the field.

The bingles' cataloguer, Maurice Gould, from whom all the examples of particular coins given above are taken, in recounting the story of the Alaskan's abortive trip to the Seattle Post Office refers to the private coins as "legal tender," appropriately in quotation marks, since they lacked the defining characteristic of legal tender, the legally conferred right to extinguish debt whether or not the creditor wanted that tender. But Gould suggests that in Alaska private money did resemble legal tender in certain respects, for it circulated everywhere and it would have been thought churlish to refuse it, as the story of the Eskimo's indignation in Seattle indicates. In other words, private money for many years remained a commonplace of the Alaskan economy, the "legal tender" of Seward's icebox while it had no other. Merchants issued it at will, their customers took it voluntarily and spent it indiscriminately. Nothing but necessity compelled its acceptance; nearly everyone, however, preferred the convenience of the distinctive little aluminum coins from the Pioneer Bar and a hundred other combination mints and watering spots to gold dust and bear skins. The advantages plainly outweighed the disadvantages.

Article 1, Section 8 of the Constitution vests in the United

States the power to "coin money and regulate the value thereof," a privilege which has been so successfully guarded for the last hundred years that the very idea of private money seems ludicrous. It was not, however, a laughing matter for the Framers; they acted in the fresh and not altogether happy memory of the deluge of tokens that constituted the only readily available change after the Revolution. Commercial speculation produced the United States' first fractional money: after 1783 businesses imported huge quantities of half-penny pieces from England, many of them from Boulton's, a well known private mint in Birmingham. Over forty tons of a single variety reached New York; it was called the Nova Constellatio after its inscription in honor of America, the "new constellation" among nations, and was said to have been ordered from England by no less a luminary than Gouverneur Morris. Another such piece carried a replica of the insignia displayed by the old continental buttons. Peter Getz (or Götz), an ingenious German who lived in Lancaster, Pennsylvania, built one of the first American fire engines and minted one of the first American coins bearing George Washington's likeness.

To an Annapolis goldsmith named Chalmers, who entered the money business in 1783, goes the honor of coining the first American silver: shillings, sixpences, and threepences. Previously, Spanish dollars cut into eight pieces or "bits" constituted most of the country's large change, but the skill of frontier alchemists in extracting nine, or even ten, pieces of "eight" from a single dollar made Chalmers' coins popular.

Some of these preconstitutional coins carried advertising; most were anonymously issued and hence could not be redeemed. With the exception of occasional ventures such as Chalmers', oversupply and nonconvertibility made them undesirable, though financial historians, pointing out the necessity for some circulating medium in the new country, attribute the tokens' inconvenience to their volume rather than to their extragovernmental character. The theory that if coining a little money is a good thing, coining more is even better had its practitioners long before modern times, by no means all of them heads of state.

The mintmasters of the 1780's can, then, backhandedly claim some of the credit for the money clause of the Constitution. But over the years the government's fractional money operation has cured glut with famine, and sometimes hampered the economy as much as its predecessors had. "Coining money" must have become an expression suggesting easy work before 1789, since the country has suffered for the better part of its history from a coin shortage of greater or lesser magnitude.

A coin shortage creates a crisis the maddening intransigence of which an abstract discussion cannot convey. Only recall the magnitude of the inconvenience worked by the short supply of dimes and quarters in many American cities, particularly large ones, in 1964. Like other familiar phenomena that are taken for granted, a coin did more than facilitate a dozen simple acts a day; it was the *sine qua non* of each of them. The lack of a dime could turn a petty inconvenience into an unmitigated calamity more quickly than a whammy. An American with all the facilities of AT&T at his disposal, if he did not also have a dime, could not call Brooklyn on a bet. He could not park his car even if he found a space. Without dimes and quarters he could not tip. Within a few years, in many communities he would not have been able to ride home on a bus.

Remembering the hardship worked by a coin shortage, next imagine that certain denominations of coin simply disappear from circulation. In other words, when you did not have a penny or a nickel or a dime, you could not buy something that cost $1.16, unless you were willing to take an IOU for eighty-four cents, or the merchant was willing to reduce his price sixteen cents. That state of affairs very nearly has recurred several times in our history; small coinage has for one reason or another dried up, making it difficult for the consumer to carry on the simplest day-to-day transactions.

Yet manifestly, consumption could not merely grind to a halt and wait in a state of super-cooled deamination for the government to get out a fresh supply of small coins. The result was predictable, but still comes as a jolt when encountered in somber volumes of monetary history.

People made their own money. They made it, wrote it, stamped it, or cut it out as the case might be. They made it in whatever quantity suited the need or the impulse of the moment, out of whatever medium they found most convenient, and emblazoned it with whatever device, portrait or motto they fancied. They passed it on to whoever would take it and then made some more. Not only did the United States have a private coinage, it had dozens, at one point hundreds, of private coinages simultaneously.

The name "Higley" leads all the rest in the roll of American mintmasters, but tradition has preserved little more than the name, and even that remains uncertain, because some of Higley's supposed creations are inscribed "Granby." Whoever he was, he mined copper in Connecticut and, with the raw material so readily available, about 1737 began to manufacture coins to turn his copper to account. It is said Higley patronized the local ordinary frequently, and paid the considerable price of his thirst with homemade coppers at the rate of threepence apiece. Over two hundred years of American mintmasters have maintained the tradition of fondness for liquid refreshment begun by Higley; his capacity after a while made his piles of copper quite unwelcome at the inn, unwelcome, at least, at the rate of threepence a token. Higley proposed neither to give up drinking for lack of the score, nor to take up conventional money when he could make his own more cheaply, so settled on an expedient that seems natural enough on reflection. He lowered the "price" or denomination of his coppers. In fact, he abandoned it altogether, and struck coins labelled only, "Value me as you please/I am good copper." Then, presumably, Higley and the Connecticut publican struck a bargain for "good copper," and all imbibed happily ever after. So, in any event, the story goes, and surviving coins do bear the curious inscriptions. It suggests at least that a free enterprise mintmaster has no more of a guaranteed market for his wares than a peddler; both must give the public something it wants, at a price it considers advantageous, a price which, in the case of Higley's coins, may have been renegotiated at every transfer. Later they came to be widely accepted as the equivalent of two shillings sixpence, a rate of exchange which indicates the innkeeper may have driven a harder bargain with old Higley than either knew.

In the throes of the Napoleonic wars England's merchants set an example Brother Jonathan followed on and off for the next hundred years. Shopkeepers suffering a coin famine devised an ingenious substitute for change that may have originated with a ledger notation or promissory note. If a customer would accept an IOU for a shilling sixpence, might he not as well accept a smaller standardized IOU, a token IOU? He might, and did, gladly, for often he could spend the token much more easily than he could discount (sell) the IOU. In fact, a good supply of such tokens provided an ideal tonic for the local economy; they took the place of the government's vanished change.

Just how successfully they did so may be gauged by the reaction of the populace. The citizens of one town assembled and voted a resolution of thanks to the men who had issued the small change locally, and gratitude seems to have been the prevailing sentiment. When government coins eventually became available again, the private issues were for the most part redeemed.

Shortly after these events, Henry Drummond, Earl of Liverpool, puzzled over the "principles of currency" the coin famine had illustrated. He found instruction on more than economics, and ultimately saw an almost metaphysical meaning in the incident. The people, he believed, possessed a latent capacity for self-help, which needed only the stimulus of necessity to be put in motion. The shortage of coins had demonstrated they could cope with even as awkward a problem as the money supply. A few years later, events in America made his thesis seem prophetic.

Here the first great rash of postconstitutional privately coined money, often referred to as "hard-times tokens," appeared as a result of the financial vicissitudes of the 1830's. Andrew Jackson's attack on the Bank of the United States, culminating in the suspension of specie payments, ultimately drove most of the nation's silver coinage out of circulation, but the development only served to provoke the resourcefulness of those whose livelihoods required a supply of change.

Some one hundred sixty-four turnpike companies, canal operators, bridge proprietors, and plain storekeepers began to dispense their own privately minted copper coins. The coins represented a debt owed by whoever issued them to whoever held them, much as a modern corporation's commercial paper adds to the money supply without unduly enriching the issuer. As long as there was no other small change available, there was no incentive to redeem the tokens; they were used over and over again and became, functionally, money.

"Not one cent, but just as good," one of the tokens explained, more in deference to the counterfeiting laws than to its recipients' curiosities. The legend spoke half the truth, for the tokens served a twofold purpose: first and most obviously, making change; but second, and perhaps not entirely incidentally, promulgating the minter's political views, which, in the midst of the depression, were likely to be decidedly acidic. Andrew Jackson, particularly, found himself portrayed in a manner that a head of state could hardly relish. The medium itself constituted a reproach to his financial policies: the mere existence of private coinage served to reprimand him for his treatment of the Bank of the United States. The medium conveyed that message forcefully enough, without the addition of effigy.

A particularly popular motif on the tokens was a long-eared jackass, inscribed LLD in scorn of Jackson's honorary but incongruous degree from Harvard. The Jackson donkey thus travelled far and wide and so impressed itself on the generation's politics that it has ever after remained the symbol of the Democratic Party. The indignant Whigs' private money became enough a part of the national scene to contribute in large part to the permanent addition of the donkey to our national symbology.

President Jackson must have appreciated the more pedestrian merchants who devoted the faces of their coins to advertisements for their wares, thus deriving a double benefit from the tokens' circulation. Perhaps those who touted such things as "Phalon's New and Splendid Style of Hair Cutting" instead of the incumbent's supposed asininity were Democrats. One firm developed its new money business into an international trade, producing coins for Brazil, Liberia, and Santo Domingo, while others, such as J. M. L. and W. H. Scovill, of Waterbury, Connecticut, manufacturers of buttons, evolved a truly synergistic combination of enterprises. Perceiving a chance to harness New England technology to political exigency, the company turned part of its button works into a vast mint, produced some coins advertising their own "Gilt buttons of every description," and minted many others on order from merchants throughout the East. If a Yankee could make buttons he could make money, or preferably both, for the duration of the emergency.

German names keep popping up in the history of America's private mints, perhaps because of a Teutonic metallurgical tradition going back to the fifteenth-century Fuggers. "Dollar" itself descends from the German "thaler," and a German immigrant from Baden named Christopher Bechtler struck the first American gold dollar at his mint in Rutherfordton, North Carolina, eighteen years before the United States followed suit.

Bechtler became a mintmaster in an attempt to diversify his jewelry and watchmaking business, and since he was a renowned gunsmith as well, a case could be made for classifying his business as an early American conglomerate. In 1830 he and his son Augustine arrived at Rutherfordton, then a city in the heart of the largest gold-producing area in the United States, western North Carolina. The "money" of Rutherfordton consisted mainly of bags of gold dust passed over the counter from miner to shopkeeper in exchange for the week's supplies, for the nearest federal mint was Philadelphia. Its emissions reached North Carolina in a quantity too small to provide a circulating medium, and the miners for their part were not about to travel to Philadelphia in order to have their gold dust coined. In short, there was a need and a demand for money in North Carolina, but no supply.

The situation was ready-made for Christopher Bechtler. Hardly a year after reaching Rutherfordton he advertised in the *North Carolina Spectator and Western Advertiser* that he was prepared to coin $2.50 and $5.00 gold pieces for a fee, and within nine years he and his son had minted nearly two and one-quarter million dollars in gold. That volume testified to the need for and popularity of his business. Bechtler, in a sense, undersold the mint: he provided more dollars for the same amount of gold. Therefore, as long as his dollars circulated on a par with United States dollars—which they always did, so great was the community's confidence in his honesty—a miner literally got more for his money at Bechtler's. Mr. R. M. Patterson, Director of the United States Mint, understated the facts when he suggested to the President that it must "be more advantageous to the miner to carry his bullion to the private rather than the public mint." Word of his operation reached as far as Lysander Spooner, who, it will be recalled, argued that if Bechtler could constitutionally coin money, Spooner's American Letter Mail Company should certainly be able to carry letters constitutionally.

Bechtler spoke his native tongue until the end of his life and indulged a certain mysticism, which his neighbors recalled long after, while his nephew, who carried on the business, habitually drank two or three or four glasses of beer before breakfast, again with lunch, and still again at the end of the day. The incongruity of these quintessential Germans suddenly set down in the North Carolina back country could not have escaped their clientele. But the superstitious old man and his successors supplied the whole region with the only coinage it regularly knew for many years. One native of the area recalled that he was sixteen before he ever saw another coin. The disinterest of Bechtler's nephew and the discovery of gold in California combined to end the North Carolina business, but the coins circulated long afterwards and many found their way West in the emigrations of the 1850's. In fact, until comparatively recent times, the 1920's, Bechtler dollars were accepted by local North Carolina banks on a par with "official" money.

Bechtler coined money for profit; to be precise, 2½ percent of the bullion that passed through his hands. Despite the volume of his business, he never accumulated great wealth, and his honesty became a local proverb. His business catered to an urgent local need; some circulating money was indispensable. Perhaps it drew attention to the problem as well, for in 1837, after the German had been in business for six years, the United States opened a mint in Charlotte, with which Bechtler thereafter successfully competed.

Only legislative accident kept Bechtler out of jail. Although the private striking of copper coins constituted counterfeiting, for some reason the same rule did not apply to privately minted gold and silver. That oversight has long since been corrected, and he who would privately ameliorate a coin shortage today must answer to the Treasury. The rule presumably protects the public, and the Treasury's present-day statutory monopoly rests on stronger ground than fear that the money business might be lost to an organization providing superior service. But Bechtler's story provides reasonable cause for just such a fear:

North Carolina miners preferred Bechtler's to the Philadelphia, or even the Charlotte mint, and it would seem no one ever lost a cent on a Bechtler dollar.

Bechtler's equipment now appropriately belongs to museums. It probably never occurs to those who stumble on his dies in the North Carolina Hall of History in Raleigh, or his press at the American Numismatic Society in New York, that those artifacts were for many years the instruments for a beneficent and successful challenge by a mystical German to the most uncontroversial of all the government's monopolies.

The most memorable heyday of the private mintmaster came twenty years later with the Civil War. By then the course of events had been repeated often enough to be predictable. Wartime strains and disruptions created an inflation that made the copper in a cent worth substantially more than one one-hundredth of a dollar, partly because war industries needed copper and partly because inflation made a dollar bill less valuable. Pennies consequently disappeared from circulation; they were worth more as copper than as pennies, and so might be melted down or hoarded against the day when copper would command an even higher price. The United States Mint rapidly lost ground to Gresham's law and completely failed to keep the country supplied with small change. A. Ludewig, a Pittsburgh tobacco dealer, concisely explained the economic situation around the circumference of his own coin: "Coppers 20 pr ct premium." M. Mendel Shafer, Cincinnati "attorney and counselor at law," considered the situation deplorable enough to justify inclusion in a one-sentence summary of his political credo inscribed on his own penny: "The federal government, a national currency, free trade, and human rights."

By the fall of 1862 the situation had become desperate; the supply of small change simply did not suffice for trade. The government resorted to all sorts of expedients in a futile attempt to supply the deficiency, such as the encased postage stamps familiar to collectors, but all the stopgaps together failed to supply enough coins to keep alive the normal citizen's day-to-day economic transactions. A barter economy lay in prospect.

Enter now, like the Fifth Cavalry, a host of private mintmasters to rescue the country from the spectacle of housewives using eggs for small change or taking pinches of salt from their local grocers when their purchases fell a little short of an even dollar figure. Literally thousands (for seven to eight thousand varieties have been catalogued and many other types must have percolated briefly through local economies across the country and then vanished forever) of individuals set up shop and issued their own coins. One collection, now preserved at Lehigh University, contained 5,000 varieties, 1,358 from Ohio, 914 from New York, 511 from Michigan, 385 from Wisconsin, 270 from Indiana, 160 from Illinois, 156 from Pennsylvania, and 130 from Rhode Island. Cincinnati entrepreneurs alone accounted for 888 varieties, and generally the tokens gained greatest acceptance in the West. In fact, certain sections of the country, such as Michigan, which had theretofore hardly been reached by government coinage, experienced their first exposure to metallic currency through the private issues.

"They were undoubtedly a source of great relief and convenience," conclude two experts, George Hetrich and Julius Guttag, and that understates their contribution. In many places private money was the only money, and except for private money people would have had to take IOU's for change or go without. At least twenty-five million pieces were struck, and estimates range up to fifty million: five hundred thousand dollars worth of pennies, a quantity which shows how universally they circulated. They became the nation's principal metallic currency for over a year, from late 1862 to the end of 1863.

The ubiquity of the private penny can also be gauged from the advertisements that often appeared on it; it seems as if almost every commercial establishment in the United States doing as much as $2,500 a year in trade became a mint as well, or rather, the customer of a local mint that produced coins for merchants for miles around, such as W. K. Lamphear, "manufacturer of metallic cards," who inserted his advertisement on the reverse of a coin produced for his clients, "L. Phil Meredith and J. N. M'Clung, dentists at M'Clung's dental rooms" in Cincinnati. No shop was too small to boast its own token. A Cincinnati barber put out pieces good for one shave. Joseph Zanone's ice cream saloon in Springfield, Illinois, and Randal's photographic gallery alike enjoyed their own money. Senour's Drug Store in Indianapolis offered coins good for "One Glass Soda

Water," while John W. Lee, of Lexington, Kentucky, circulated tokens good for one half-pint of milk, one pint, a half-gallon, and a gallon. A particularly impecunious merchant might share a token with a neighbor and thus halve the cost to himself; a Zanesville, Ohio, specimen touts Barrell's Worm Confections on one side and Cary's CCC Cough Cure on the other.

Someone (Parker?) in Indianapolis assured whoever came into possession of his issues that "Parker's Shirts Will Fit." A lawyer in Lyons, Michigan, had either the good luck to be named A. Button or the imagination to adopt that pseudonym —coins were sometimes called buttons, perhaps because button factories had manufactured them—which he inscribed on his tokens with the announcement that he was a "War claim attorney and general collecting agent." Insurance agents, hair restorers, grindstone agents, and stereoscopic picture vendors all climbed aboard the bandwagon, as did butchers, stove sellers, liquor dealers, and furniture stores.

Certain members of the medical profession were not above taking advantage of the advertising potential of private money, and one anticipated the Burma Shave technique of serial cards by half a century. He began on a low key: "If you get sick use Dr. Bennett's medicines." Another coin proclaimed that "200,-000 families now use Dr. Bennett's medicines," while a third grandiosely heralded, "50,000 persons annually cured by Dr. Bennett's medicines" (history does not record whether the figure was based on an actual headcount or the more economical form of analysis effected by dividing by four and assuming one hundred percent efficacy). "Teeth Extracted Without Pain," bragged dentist B. P. Belknap. Dr. L. C. Rose of Detroit assumed a more dignified pose, befitting his specialty: "Dr. L. C. Rose treats all chronic female and venereal diseases."

The use of tokens by small tradesmen did not mean that they were eschewed by more substantial dealers. A steamship company used the face of one of its issues to distribute its timetables far and wide. In the spring of 1863, when the idea of private pennies first reached New York from the West, a New York saloonkeeper named G. Lindenmuller began to make change with his own money, and before the exigency passed had managed to circulate ten thousand dollars worth of one-cent copper coins, each bearing his bearded Teutonic visage on one side and an inviting stein on the other. Lindenmuller apparently set a record, but huge numbers of other types also circulated, especially one simply inscribed "Army and Navy."

The "Army and Navy" cents were the most numerous representatives of a group that devoted its space to political sloganeering, reminiscent of the Jackson era. A particularly popular gambit was to incorporate "not one cent" somewhere in the design to avoid the possibility of running afoul of the counterfeiting laws, and at the same time (by putting the "not" in very small letters) indicate the denomination. "Millions for defense, not ONE CENT for tribute," one inscription ran, while another substituted a cynical variant: "Millions for contractors, not ONE CENT for widows." Anti-Administration sentiment found vent in coins with General McClellan's portrait.

John Adams Dix, while Secretary of the United States Treasury in 1861, concerned himself with the problem of returning to United States custody certain vessels under the command of Confederate sympathizers. In this connection he instructed his deputy, Hemphill Jones, to forward to a lieutenant on a United States cutter orders to arrest a Captain Breshwood and if necessary to treat him as a mutineer; "If anyone attempts to haul down the American flag," Dix stated, "shoot him on the spot." The peremptory command caught the national mood at a responsive pitch, and Dix became a front-page personality overnight. Capitalizing on this popularity, many varieties of private tokens pictured an American flag with the legend, "The flag of our union 1863," and on the obverse the famous words, "If anyone attempts to haul down the American flag, shoot him on the spot," surrounding DIX in large capitals. Thousands of these pennies brought Dix's name before the few who had not already heard it, and kept his phrase alive in the memories of those who had. Dix rode his renown to the governorship of New York in 1872, assisted in at least some degree by the universal use of the private coppers that had been issued as a speculation.

Speculations, private profit-making ventures, are exactly what the patriotic issues were, for while a man could always, for instance, take F. Behr's token to his saloon in Detroit and quaff "Ein glass Bier," the sloganeering coins did not carry the names of their issuers and so could not be redeemed at all if they would not pass in trade. In his 1863 Annual Report, the Director of the United States Mint advised that the coins on the average contained copper worth about one-fifth cent, so if enough could be anonymously circulated there was a potential for a substantial profit. Of course, F. Behr might have hoped for an advantageous arrangement, too, even though his coins bore his name; the homonymous bear holding aloft a beer mug in his right paw might have tempted the saloonist's customers to retain the token as a souvenir, a memory in their pocket and money in Behr's. Or the guaranteed redeemability at Behr's might have brought them back another day to spend their change at Behr's rather than at a competitor's. Finally, even if they spent the token elsewhere, its circulation would advertise Behr's beer wherever it travelled. In short, private money brought dividends to tradesmen as well as anonymous patriots, and after all, one of the coins insisted, "Money makes the mare go." One mystifying product of the C. Magnus National Printing Establishment announced that "100 entitles to a $2 view of New York City"; whatever that scheme involved, it no doubt left C. Magnus a little richer. Perhaps with an eye on impending government suppression (but more likely in an outburst of Copperheadism), another coin pleaded "Live and Let Live."

That the Director of the Mint was unwilling to do. His 1863 report conveyed his indignation at the supposed 400 percent profit the speculators made every time they placed a fifth-cent penny in circulation. This considerably overestimated the rewards of mintmastering, for aside from the price of the copper, the entrepreneurs had to cover the costs of dies and other expenses attendant upon the tokens' manufacture, estimated by one expert—Falkner—at seventy-five cents a hundred. And there was always the final difficulty of introducing the morale-boosting product into circulation; however edifying the sentiment behind "Death to Traitors" or "Union Forever" coins might be, only a finite number could be passed. In normal times even real pennies have limited marketability above a certain number. If unlimited quantities of the speculators' issues had come on the market, they would have been refused on all sides, but as the Director of the Mint pointed out with profound distress, "they were freely used as coin by the public." To a numismatist of 1875, they "admirably represented the fervor that

animated every breast, and made heroes of farmers and me-
chanics," but they "admirably represent" something else as
well: the success of private imagination, incised and disguised
with slogans like "The Boys in Blue," in making a profit by
mitigating a national want created by the ineptitude of the
government monopoly. The government allowed the coin shortage to exist as long as it did because it felt that coins must have
an intrinsic value approaching their face value to gain acceptance, although that notion was being refuted every day in
every city in the North by the freely circulating privately issued tokens.

The acceptability of the tokens may be gauged by the celer-
ity with which they passed from hand to hand; although in
actual use for little over a year, many surviving specimens are
worn, scratched, or bent, while infrequently circulated numbers are rare enough to command premium prices (hardly any
private Civil War penny in any condition can be bought for less
than a dollar). Collectors wax baroquely ecstatic over this kind
of item: "Many a desirable gem lies hid for months—perhaps
years—in a dark corner of some junk shop, among a lot of rusty
nails, and a miscellaneous gathering of brass and copper, ac-
cumulating as rapidly with film and verdigris as it increases in
rarity and value, doomed never to meet the cheering eye of a
virtuoso and to receive in its old age his welcome hand, his fond
embrace, his fostering care."

Still, it cannot be said that tokens were universally hon-
ored, even by their issuers; it is related that the Third Avenue
Railroad in New York requested the jolly German Lindenmuller to redeem a large number of his tokens, but the saloonkeeper laughingly refused. Relatively few such stories have
survived, however, and it is as significant that the Third Avenue Railroad should have quantities of Lindenmuller cents on
hand as it is that Lindenmuller declined to redeem them, since
the anecdote shows the tokens circulated as money and not just
as chits for merchandise from a particular dealer. Of course,
the anonymous issues, something like one-fifth of the total, had
to pass from hand to hand as money or not at all.

For the most part, the tokens seemed to serve their purpose
well. Although they could have theoretically constituted a total

loss for whoever finished last in the nationwide game of hot
potato, the public seemed to welcome and even relish them.
When government change finally began to come back into circulation in 1863, the use of private issues continued on a large
scale; in fact, they reached their period of greatest popularity
at a time when the shortage that inspired them had been substantially alleviated, and only legislation coupled with government prosecutions finally succeeded in ending their career. For
a year or more the tokens contributed mightily to the health of
local economies all over the North, having appeared when the
need arose with a spontaneous success that was gratifying then
and is undeservedly forgotten today.

During the Depression, people once again were forced to
provide their own money when government supplies dried up.
Their issues bear witness to the humor with which they faced
their predicament: "rubber checks" made out of rubber, and
"dam script" illustrated with a prodigious Columbia River dam.
These were not make-do IOU's but real money substitutes; at
least one court ruled alimony could be paid with the script.
*Collier's* called the token money "a magnificent testimonial to
the courage, imagination, and resourcefulness of the American
people." Of course, it was also illegal, clearly violating the Civil
War law. The government, however, indicated its own opinion
of the wisdom of the law by not bringing any prosecutions
against the Depression mintmasters.

Most commentators on private money, including those who
have recognized its utility, agree that it has been primarily
important as an expedient and a stopgap rather than as a permanent alternative to legal tender. Nevertheless, the history of
private coinage retains a quixotic fascination for students of
government monopolies, for time and again some unlikely local has turned himself into a mintmaster overnight, sometimes
with surprisingly propitious results. The issuers' adventures
make good reading if not necessarily satisfactory paradigms
for solution of present-day problems.

The desirability and, ideally, the superiority of a government coinage, however, do not self-evidently dictate the present statutory monopoly over items "intended to be used as
money." From the first this has sounded like a fairly silly

antiwampum law, notwithstanding the longstanding tradition of seignorage. The statute's earliest recorded application offended the common sense of the judge who tried the case. The Monongahela Bridge Company and various other enterprises, faced with the continuing shortage of coins, used tickets inscribed "good for one trip" to make change. Although the practice seemed clearly to violate the terms of the statute, and the judge said as much in so many words, he chose to interpret it away with a nonjudicial fillip: "From our knowledge of the gentlemen having the management of these companies, we are satisfied they entertain no desire to abuse [their corporate privileges]." The indictment was dismissed.

Very possibly the judge's practically extrastatutory opinion is all that makes it legally possible for today's bus companies to issue script for change, a practice annoying to customers but hardly subversive of the nation's money supply.

Enforcement activity seems as frivolous now as it was in 1863. William F. Rickenbacker has collected some examples of merchants who tried to help alleviate their own problems arising from the coin shortage of 1964 by issuing various money substitutes. The Jewel Tea Company proposed to issue script in one-cent, five-cent, and ten-cent denominations to make change for its customers; Krogers, too, planned to resort to a similar expedient. In Monroe, Wisconsin, the First National Bank actually paid out $400 for the manufacture of 20,000 wooden nickels to be used as small change. A Nantucket merchant minted his own coins embellished with an imperious whale. The United States Treasury, however, frowned on all these palliative enterprises and threatened some of their perpetrators with prosecution if they did not desist, a stance that reduces the monopoly to comic-opera dimensions indeed. So far as the leading cases reveal, the only remotely salutary application of the century-old law ever to see court was against an amusement park operator whose tokens, stamped "good for amusement only," were being misused as slugs in vending machines. But the government lost because the slugs could not realistically be considered money. With no more than a few wooden nickels to its credit, the statute seems more a weapon for Mouse-That-Roared harassment than an instrument of seriously considered public policy.

A convention of the ghosts of the hundreds of private American mintmasters, from hard-drinking old Higley to the still corporeal Mr. Gilroy Roberts (whom the Franklin Mint of Philadelphia–which does not produce money but souvenir coins–lured away from Uncle Sam a few years ago), would be a backslapping, morris-dancing affair with quantities of beer quenching any sense of somber public service. The likes of Lindenmuller made money to make money, not to serve their fellow citizens, and the very desire for gain that motivated America's mintmasters guaranteed that they would circulate their product only when the public's necessities furnished an outlet. The irony of the coinage monopoly is that it almost never requires enforcement except when something goes wrong and the resulting complications make private money particularly useful.

ⓞⓞⓞⓞⓞⓞ

# CHAPTER FOUR

# An Education
# of Choice

IN CHICAGO A THOUSAND TEENAGERS DROP OUT OF
school each month; at any given time there are about 47,000
young people out of school and out of work in that city alone.
In Harlem the out-of-school, out-of-work population is estimated to be 70,000. According to a 1964 survey cited by President Johnson, sixty percent of tenth-grade students from low
income areas of the United States' fifteen largest cities will not
graduate from high school; in New York City, sixty-five percent
of the Negro and Puerto Rican students drop out before graduation. These statistics were collected in the Fall 1968 issue of the
*Carnegie Quarterly* in an attempt to measure the quantifiable
failures of urban public schools, failures which have in the last
five years gained almost universal recognition. Less subject to
quantification and therefore slower to gain notoriety are the
same schools' qualitative deficiencies, their defects of mind
and soul. Public schools in poverty areas often do not even
pretend to an educational justification; they are merely a
means, and an expensive one, of keeping kids off the street for
a few years. A dropout retained for two or three extra years of
custodial care is no victory for education. Public schools may

promise, as Jonathan Kozol bitterly summarized, only "death at an early age" to those they do keep in.

Educators have devoted countless mind-racking hours to the problems of improving such schools, and a solution is increasingly becoming a political necessity as well as an educational one. The Bundy Plan for decentralization of the New York City public schools was a notorious attempt to reorganize school administration in order to meet the needs and interests of both students and parents. In the words of the Bundy report, the goal was to "create within New York City a school system that in imagination, flexibility and innovation could match or surpass the most dynamic suburban or small-city school district in the country." The rosy expectations in retrospect measure the disaster of the decentralization experiment better than all the denunciation poured on it by its critics. Lack of flexibility and resistance to innovation among members of the United Federation of Teachers and elsewhere in fact became hallmarks of the debacle.

Yet outside the framework of the public school system there have been more successful attempts to meet the needs of youngsters previously relegated to a custodial education. In New York, in Chicago, and in Boston, private schools have made it possible for kids to opt out of the pattern of failure that seems as endemic to slum-district public schools as to the slums themselves.

For whatever reasons–professional, bureaucratic, or racial–many blacks are sure that their children are not receiving an even barely adequate education in public schools, and that the reason so many drop out has more to do with the schools than with any inherent black laziness or stupidity. Even for the exceptionally talented, the incentives of getting ahead economically or pulling out of the slums are counteracted by the frustration of being steered into nonacademic courses and graduating with a general degree, appropriately viewed by colleges as a certificate of unreadiness for higher education. And many blacks, with the majority of other Americans, have come to look on a college education as an essential, nearly magical, ingredient of success, whether it leads them out into The Man's world or back into the slums to improve life there. Those motivated and talented enough for college but held back by public schools have received the most attention and the most sympathy, but American education has long purported to develop the potential and talents of any student, no matter how little inclined or suited to Latin and algebra. A purely custodial school is as unrewarding to kids who have no idea of ever going to college as to those who do. A keep-them-off-the-streets educational system impartially straitjackets everyone.

Urban blacks consequently are resorting in increasing numbers to private schools to provide the kind of education they think they need, as opposed to the kind a public system thinks they should have or feels it must offer out of necessity. Started by individuals who recognize the potential of black students and understand the frustration of trying to get ahead through the public school system, the black private schools have enjoyed signal success. Only in part can this be attributed to improvements in educational technique, such as reduction of the teacher-student ratio; the basic explanation is the natural fact that the private black schools have enough respect for their charges to assume that they are capable of academic achievement. Their faith is quickly communicated to the students themselves, and it generates in the students a confidence and pride that are incompatible with the syndrome of failure so characteristic of city public schools.

The black private schools' regenerative mission plays a variation on the traditional theme of private schools in America, and like their forerunners, they cater to the special needs of a group that does not consider itself adequately served by the public schools. Secondary and primary education, after all, has been a *de facto* state monopoly in this country only since the second half of the nineteenth century, and even then only in some communities. Elsewhere, the tradition of private schools, begun long before the Revolution by the Congregational and Anglican churches, survived, along with scattered nondenominational, free enterprise academies dating back to the mid-eighteenth century. For the wealthy these provided an alternative to public schools, and their successors today in some urban areas such as Washington, D.C., serve an even larger constituency: everyone who can possibly afford to take his children out of the universally calumniated public schools. When big-city blacks became dissatisfied with the public schools, seeking to establish a private alternative was a most American thing to do.

Perhaps the closest analogue to the black schools now operating in Boston, New York and Chicago is not Groton or St. Paul's, but the multitude of Quaker academies set up by Friends chary of the dilution of religious and moral principles their children might suffer as a result of attending public schools. In their own schools Quakers could provide a "guarded education," guarded, that is, from the domination of what they saw as an alien side of American culture. Similar feelings lay behind Amish schools, and at least in part motivated the establishment of the vast system of Catholic primary and secondary education, and the largest Protestant school system–that of the Lutherans. A minority fearing absorption or, at best, corruption by the majority who controlled the public schools tried in each case to escape homogenization by starting schools of its own. The sentiments of those who patronize and support the black schools are not necessarily as separatist as those of the Amish or Quakers, but like the supporters of sectarian schools, blacks do not want their children systematically crunched into cubes of scrap steel like so many junked cars by a system whose objects and priorities are not the same as their own.

Among the oldest and most successful of the black programs are those sponsored by the Urban League of Greater New York. Housed in storefronts, mostly in Harlem and the Lower East Side of New York City, Street Academies are schools that provide a grade school education for dropouts of all ages from public schools. In addition to three teachers with college degrees, the staff of each academy consists of three streetworkers who go out and persuade dropouts to give school another try. The 120 streetworkers (70 of them black) almost always live in the neighborhood where they work; besides bringing kids into the storefronts, they encourage and counsel them along the way: some even provide apartments for their homeless protégés. The number of storefronts in operation at any given time varies, but always some stress job training or starting youths in local businesses, some concentrate on recreation and counseling, one works with dope addicts, and around ten offer formal academic instruction.

Each storefront has from ten to thirty students who stay

from six weeks to a year. The academic curriculum emphasizes math and reading, often remedial, but there are also sessions of African and black history, and sometimes Arabic or Swahili. "Sociology" classes try to get the kids to clarify their feelings about Harlem and think about ways around problems of the slums. They worry, for example, about whether going away to college and finding a career elsewhere is the answer, or whether they should come back and try to improve the situation in Harlem, as many Street Academy graduates have done (increasing numbers of streetworkers in the program are Street Academy grads).

Joseph Featherstone interviewed one student who contrasted the Street Academy with the public schools he had known. One of the things that turned the boy from the public schools was the apparent irrelevance of the subject matter; he did not think George Washington had much to say to him. He was contemptuous of teachers who were "always trying to make deals with the kids, where you could study or not, just so long as you didn't make trouble." And he had been disturbed by police disguised as students lurking all over the building. At the Street Academy, he was proud to be studying academic college preparatory subjects, and proud that teachers expected more from him than trouble, even including homework. Though the teaching methods used in the Street Academies are conventional, they are not merely custodial.

Money for the Street Academies' program comes from varied sources, most of them private. The Ford Foundation has made substantial grants; the city and the Neighborhood Youth Corps have also contributed. Benefits have helped, such as a college football game in February 1969–the Football Coaches Foundation and P. Ballantine & Sons contributed $25,000 of the gate receipts. And recently Harv Oostdyk, the white former streetworker who started the program, recruited a number of large companies—IBM, Time-Life, Celenese, and the First National City Bank among them—to support one academy each, at an approximate cost per academy of $50,000 a year.

When the students graduate from the Street Academies they enter an Academy of Transition, where they are exposed to a more systematically academic program. After attaining the equivalent of an eighth- or ninth-grade education, about ninety percent of the Street and Transition Academy graduates have gone on to Harlem Prep or Newark Prep.

A conventional private school of sixty years' standing, Newark Prep at first took a few of the brightest Street Academy graduates bussed from Harlem. Now it accepts about eighty every year, and the recruits from Harlem constitute a majority of its student body. The curriculum is standard, but classes are conducted quite formally, unlike those in the academies. In 1968 twenty-seven Street Academy alumni who finished at Newark went on to college.

Harlem Prep, a school opened by the Urban League in the fall of 1967, was specifically designed to continue the Street Academies program. Housed first in an old armory located on the Harlem River, the school in its first year accepted seventy out of three hundred applicants, who could have been attracted by its convenience if nothing else; central Harlem, with a population of 300,000, did not have a single public high school. The League persuaded Edward Carpenter, a Negro guidance counselor with the New York Board of Education, to accept the job of headmaster. In addition to Carpenter, there are four Negro teachers, and three white nuns from Manhattanville College in Purchase, New York, which volunteered the services of the nuns and pays them.

In its second year of operation the school expanded to accommodate about one hundred twenty students, many of them applicants from the public schools, and moved into a converted Harlem supermarket purchased partly with money from the Sheila Mosser Foundation. Money for operating expenses came from the Astor, Hayden, and Arwood Foundations; the school has since been helped by contributions from industry and private individuals. The budget for the first year was about $300,-000, or over $4,000 per pupil, a figure far surpassing that of the New York or, for that matter, any other public school system. No tuition is charged.

The students, aged sixteen to twenty-five, spend the bulk of their time on math and English, and, as in the Street Academies, studying academic subjects is a source of pride. Writing skills are particularly stressed. The curriculum includes African history and black literature. Students also read Plato and practice the Socratic method. Classes are conducted like seminars, with ample opportunity for discussion. Like the traditional prep school students, the boys and girls at Harlem Prep wear school blazers, and have a school motto, flag, newspaper, basketball team, and choir. But the emblems on their blazers are of their own design: African shields with crossed spears, inscribed with two Swahili words, *Moja* (union) and *Logo* (brotherhood). Students themselves agreed on the rules, which ban swearing and, out of respect to the nuns, hats. If they are punctual, perform certain services to the community, and earn grades of 85 or above, they receive $25 a week.

In June 1968 twenty-seven former dropouts graduated from Harlem Prep; all had received full or partial scholarships to colleges like Wesleyan, Vassar, the University of California, Harvard, and Fordham. Fifty students attended summer school, conducted on the campus of Riverdale Country School, a traditional prep school on the outskirts of the city. Three others went to Africa for the summer, under a program sponsored by the Urban League.

At the second Harlem Prep graduation in June 1969, seventy-one students received diplomas and were accepted by thirty-seven colleges and universities. Most were former dropouts; some had graduated from vocational schools or had received general high school diplomas. Their commencement speaker, Dr. John Cave, chairman of the Medical Board of Harlem Hospital and director of its School of Anesthesiology, advised the grads to stay away from campus politics, a warning reiterated by a Harlem Prep alumnus then in college. Dr. Cave went on to advise the students to "concentrate on acquiring skills that could be of service to the people of the slums," and most of the students at present do plan to return to Harlem.

The feelings of the graduates were succinctly expressed by Charles Trahan: "Next September I will be a freshman at Wesleyan. Imagine that. Last year I was blind and lost. Now I have a scholarship."

Harlem Prep is the only one of the new black private schools that has enjoyed substantial publicity, and it is extremely difficult to gauge exactly how widely its example has been followed. The major educational periodicals have given only intermittent space to the black private school phenomenon; it therefore has to be examined almost solely through fugitive items in the press, which do, at least, demonstrate that Harlem Prep is not unique.

The change worked there in one year seems no less miraculous to others than to Charles Trahan, and the moral has not escaped, for one, the Congress of Racial Equality (CORE). It, too, now plans a private school. With the help of Long Island University, CORE plans to raise $1.25 million to buy L.I.U.'s Brooklyn College of Pharmacy. Plans call for a program to give Negro youths the equivalent of a junior college education, charging as little tuition as possible.

The Concord Baptist Church in Brooklyn, too, is sponsoring its own school. The church, in the largely black Bedford-Stuyvesant area of Brooklyn, was concerned about the steady flow of its congregation to Long Island in search of better schools–parents were worried about overcrowding and public school teachers' apparent lack of interest in their children. The church was peculiarly equipped to undertake the project because its minister, Reverend Gardner C. Taylor, formerly was a member of the Board of Education, and Reverend Taylor's wife possessed sufficient experience to develop the curriculum and written teaching materials for the elementary school. Although tuition is charged–$300 per year per pupil (of which the church pays one fourth)–there is a long waiting list, as at other private schools in Bedford-Stuyvesant. The seven-year-old school has one hundred thirty pupils in grades one through six, eight teachers, all college graduates, a ratio of twenty pupils per teacher, much lower than that of most public schools. Concentration is on reading, with emphasis on phonics instead of the "look and say" method used in public schools in New York, by which method reading becomes an exercise in memory rather than in reasoning. The improvement in reading skills among children who were well on their way to serious reading difficulties argues forcefully in favor of either phonics or private education–and perhaps the dichotomy is artificial under present conditions.

The curriculum at Concord also offers all other standard elementary-level academic subjects, plus intensive courses in black history and culture. As in the other black schools, they are taught partly for their substance but largely for the psychological boost imparted to the black students on learning of black achievements. Generations of white children grew proud of America by hearing about George Washington and Thomas Jefferson; blacks want their own pantheon, and get it in their own schools. Parents of the Concord students back the whole program but reserve their greatest enthusiasm for the strict discipline and compulsory nondenominational chapel services three times a week.

The East Harlem Block Schools represent the efforts of another group that has given up on the public schools. Parents, many of them Puerto Rican, were unhappy because their Spanish-speaking children were expected to know and use English in spite of inadequate instruction in the schools, and were tired of having their kids used as guinea pigs for various educational experiments. They shared the understandable goal of wanting their children to learn something while they were at school. With the help of foundation and government Head Start funds, four years ago they set up nursery and primary classes in four locations with a total of 135 pupils. Parents contribute $1 per week; they also elect the board of directors, make lunches and snacks, work as assistant teachers, and help in other ways. There is one professional teacher and one assistant per twelve to fifteen children, and students have learned English in a year. Most parents hope to add grades to the school year by year; until then they operate a tutoring project for older children. They would also like to find other funds to support their yearly budget of $2,000 per pupil because of the red tape and uncertainty generated by Head Start funding.

New York has been the center for these new schools, predictably enough since its school system is the largest and most troubled in the nation and since it has a huge minority group population; ethnic pluralism naturally entails educational pluralism. But other cities are beginning to pick up the idea. In Chicago an alliance of eight Protestant and Catholic churches in the West Garfield Park area has founded a high school called the CAM (Christian Action Ministry) Academy. (More than one of the new private schools includes in its name the practically archaic appellation "academy"; it avoids the unpleasant overtones of "school" and invokes the elitism of the prep school tradition.) The principal at CAM, Mary Nelson, formerly taught in a Lutheran school in East Africa. The academy was set up in an area that badly needed some community structure: until six years ago this was an all-white neighborhood, but within six months it turned into an all-black one. Although the public high school has a dropout rate of fifty to sixty percent, there is little incentive to improve this because the school is now operating at 250 percent of capacity. CAM Academy accepts dropouts, who have an average reading level a little below that of the sixth grade, but the average reading level of *graduates* of the same public high school equals that of the seventh grade.

Housed in an old bank building, the academy charges a small tuition fee, but many students work at the school to earn their tuition or have part-time jobs on the outside arranged by CAM. Students, whose average age is eighteen, can enter any time during the year. Unlike Harlem Prep, the school is not entirely college preparatory, and anyone who wants to can come. Job preparation is stressed, and toward that end courses in economics and investment are offered; students also help manage the school cafeteria and paperback bookstore. Three certificates are offered: the first signifies completion of the tenth grade and readiness for job training; the second is a high school diploma; the third shows completion of the college preparatory course.

The school is strict and no-nonsense: students who cannot or will not learn are dropped, though they can be readmitted later if they develop motivation. The rules, posted on signs, are like those of most schools: no booze or drugs, no weapons, and no swearing–"out of respect for the sisters"—but were drawn up by the students themselves. There is a wide array of electives, including art, psychology, music and photography. Afro-American history is required.

Striking evidence of the success of the academy is found in its charges' academic achievements: in twelve weeks the approximately one hundred students improved their reading ability an average of two grade levels, and their math, three. As at Harlem Prep, the accomplishment cannot be explained only in terms of a more imaginative curriculum and more dedicated teachers; it must also be attributed to the students' soaring morale. In spite of the fact that eighty-five percent of the boys had previous police records and all had spent from a month to two years on the streets, out of school and work, thirty students graduated the first year, twenty with scholarships to colleges all over the country. One boy went from a second-grade to an eighth-grade reading level in twelve weeks, and is now attending a California community college.

In Boston, parents were catalyzed to action by the firing of Jonathan Kozol, author of *Death at an Early Age*. Some parents reckoned that he had been the thirteenth teacher for the fourth graders at a school in Roxbury; while there, he had tried to work closely with his students' parents, a stance the latter approved highly. Failing to get any of their requests met–including Kozol's reinstatement, changes in curriculum and reading materials, an end to corporal punishment, and property improvements, for which they volunteered their own labor–they took matters into their own hands and started a bussing service, a step promised but not implemented by school officials. They could do so with impunity because Boston has an open enrollment plan, by which any child can go to any school in the city if there is a vacancy and parents can provide transportation. The parents hired busses during the summer to bus their kids to nonslum schools, and also, with Kozol's help, set up tutorial programs.

Starting a school of their own was a logical next step. Even though the sums of money involved were forbidding, $80,000–$100,000 a year, both black and white parents, led by Mrs. Julia Walker, started out by giving a round of benefit parties, and eventually generated enough publicity and interest to bring in other money. One woman of Boston bought an ivy-covered Revolutionary-era building in Roxbury which she offered to rent to the parents until they could buy it from her. The school started in 1966 with fifty children and funds for only a month or two of operation. But it managed to survive, with help from the Harvard Graduate School of Education and other colleges and universities in the area, and now has eighty-eight children in grades one through six. It charges $250 tuition, but scholarships are available. Parents are very much involved in planning and administration as well as fund-raising, and are doing all in their power to provide the community with an alternative to public schools. An unusual feature of the Roxbury school is an attempt to mix all economic, ethnic and educational backgrounds; the emphasis is still strongly on community spirit, but these people see themselves as part of a larger community, and have succeeded in attracting a thirty percent white enrollment.

Now a related citizens group called the Committee for Community Educational Development has received full state financial support to set up an independent school system. In addition, it won a $390,000 development grant from the Ford Foundation to help in the recruitment and training of staff. This arrangement was made possible by a 1967 act of the Massachusetts legislature that allowed for funding of private schools, and that set up an Educational Development Commission to superintend the selection of special schools and to see that they meet state educational requirements. The citizens' first school was scheduled to open in September 1969 in Roxbury; Roxbury School will have 250 pupils aged five to ten. No tuition will be charged. The school is organized to allow close participation of parents and community members, a flexible curriculum, and a wide use of nonprofessional staff. The program has been in the works for two years, and the committee ultimately plans a complete alternative network of schools for children from prekindergarten through high school, with each school located in a different area of the city but drawing pupils from the whole urban area.

The Boston school exemplifies what may be an increasingly popular synthesis: public assistance to private primary and secondary schools. Private schools, particularly parochial schools, have in recent years faced a series of financial crises aggravated by the burden on their patrons of paying taxes for public schools on top of tuition for their own. A shortage of funds has made primary and secondary education in some cities more nearly a governmental monopoly today than it was forty, or even ten, years ago. The greatest obstacles to the proliferation of black private schools are also financial. Starting and running a school obviously takes more money than most slums can raise. There is, after all, a finite market for bake-sale goods in most communities, and foundations, which have made up most of the difference for the schools examined above, cannot undertake to give everyone an alternative to public education. They do not really want to: they regard their contributions as "seed money" and are primarily interested in providing models for others to follow.

Yet black parents, like white parents, manifestly want the option of private schools. The government's monopoly of secondary education, where it exists, is not one of those enjoying the blind unthinking acceptance accorded the postal system and other government monopolies discussed in this book. Private schools are widely accepted and except for the financial barriers would be even more widely utilized. A specially commissioned Gallup Poll showed that fifty-nine percent of those responding favored nonpublic schools over public schools for their own children. The popular stereotype of private education as the prerogative of upper-class Establishmentarians does not reflect the aspirations of a majority of Americans.

This trend–more and more people disillusioned with public schools but unable to afford an alternative–has suggested to several commentators the possibility of using state tuition grants or vouchers (good for a fixed amount of money at any accredited school of the parents' choice) to continue tax support of primary and secondary education while at the same time permitting parents to utilize private schools if they so desire. In California, Assemblyman William Campbell introduced legislation to implement the voucher system, saying, "The public school system is a virtual monopoly, with all [monopoly's] inherent bureaucratic and organizational rigidity." In Massachusetts, 1967 legislation authorizes direct state financial support of private schools, and the Boston community project discussed above relies on this assistance. Pennsylvania, Rhode Island, Connecticut, and Ohio have enacted laws to aid private education. Each state was motivated primarily by a desire to save parochial schools, but the legislation could have other far-reaching effects as well.

Tuition grants raise unpleasant connotations for many because of their use (until declared unconstitutional) in Prince Edward County, Virginia, in preserving segregation. Nevertheless, from a different perspective, even that example is encouraging: Prince Edward Academy, the private white school, was not unsuccessful academically. Having been animated by an esprit perhaps akin to that which the private black schools have fostered, and having enjoyed the participation and support of white parents who previously might have felt as frozen out of public school control as black parents in Ocean Hill, New York, Prince Edward Academy provided an education superior to that available in many Southside Virginia high schools, notwithstanding its ill-starred conception.

Tuition grants or vouchers offer a far better chance to slip the toils of public education than do direct subsidies to private schools. Subsidies must be granted on the basis of some criteria, and that means administrators, reports, evaluations, enforcement proceedings, and all the other bureaucratic paraphernalia which the public system already suffers. The most liberal, anti-control legislator could not ordain it otherwise—is the state to hand out indeterminate subsidies to anything that calls itself a school? A subsidy system presupposes controls.

A tuition grant or tuition voucher system does not automatically escape them, for legislative ingenuity can burden the grant with enough conditions to make it as restrictive as the public system itself. Tuition grants, however, do not absolutely require more than the most minimal controls for their administration, since individual parents can decide what kind of education is desirable and implement that decision with the control over educational finance grants would give them. This freedom would, no doubt, produce some disconcertingly unconventional "schools," schools whose aberrations would be cited to prove that private choice in education is unworkable. But maybe aberration is what the system needs most. Who would not have looked askance at storefronts ten years ago, and who will criticize them today? If vouchers atomized education in America, and every atom traced a different track, the gain in energy would be more than worth the loss in order.

If private schools are recognized as a means of achieving specific public purposes, there should be no insuperable legal objection to tax support for them through a voucher plan or otherwise. Then as many parents as wanted could patronize schools that not only scorned city hall but also actually competed with each other for students. The record of the black private schools, in the face of the greatest educational hurdles in America, gives an idea of what may be accomplished.

Public schools are trying to learn from the grass-roots black institutions and are beginning to pay them the ultimate compliment of imitation. The success of the Urban League's Street Academies program is attested by the interest of New York City schools in it. Plans have been made for a new wing, entirely college preparatory, in Benjamin Franklin High School, to receive Street Academy grads. At the same time the high school will refer dropouts and truants to the academies, to get them back in school. Eighty Street Academy graduates will attend Benjamin Franklin; plans for similar programs with other high schools are also being explored. The Rockefeller Foundation has granted the Urban League an annual award of $200,000 to finance the program. It is difficult to predict how such a project will work, but obviously the Rockefeller Foundation is enthusiastic about the prospect of extending Street Academy methods to the public schools and increasing the number of pupils involved. The program will give academy graduates who cannot go on to Harlem Prep an alternative place to continue their education, but the inadequacies of the public schools will invariably afflict this initiative. Streetworkers may encounter the bureaucratic and administrative hangups indigenous to the New York school system. The dropouts' longstanding distrust of anything having to do with the public schools may carry over into their attitude toward the program. It remains to be seen whether streetworkers will have as much success dissuading potential dropouts as they have had with teenagers who have tried job hunting or loafing before going to the storefronts. Finally, since four of the five high schools in the program are making no apparent changes in curriculum or staff, the dropouts after graduating from the Street Academies will go back to the very environment they had previously rejected for the streets.

More than for any given educational technique, private schools stand for local control of a community's educational system. The municipal answer to this is decentralization, and in Washington, D. C., community-controlled Morgan Elementary School has so far been successful with that approach. The teachers union endorsed the school, and it is one of a very few schools in the District where scores on standardized tests rose considerably. Vandalism and truancy are much lower than in other D. C. public schools. Morgan has eight hundred pupils and is administered by a fifteen-member community board, which has stressed bringing the community into the classroom. Recently the board authorized the purchase of cameras so that pupils could go out to take pictures of things in the community and bring them in to discuss with the class, in a modified and updated "show and tell" session.

On the other hand, New York's decentralization attempts were disastrous. And another effort to improve the city schools is struggling with some of the same political vicissitudes that contributed to the dispatch of decentralization. More Effective Schools, a $10.7 million program to increase individualized, quality instruction, gained the full support of the United Federation of Teachers, unlike decentralization. But the woman responsible for coordinating the twenty-one schools and ensuring that they observe MES guidelines asserts her staff is altogether inadequate for the job; in any event, she has no authority to enforce the guidelines, and as a result the coordinator sees the schools in the four-year-old program gradually slipping back into the indifferentiable morass they started from. The Deputy Superintendent of Schools, who does have enforcement authority, is not alarmed; the *New York Times* quoted his remark that if school superintendents do not abide by the guidelines, he will "work on" them. The dispute is of no special significance in itself; probably every big-city school system in the country teems with similar controversies; they are the meat and drink of administrators. However bent on reform, public education seems fated to fiddle regardless of what burns.

Christopher Jencks, in a widely noted *New York Times Magazine* article, considered decentralization as an alternative to private schools and concluded it could not accomplish as much. In most of the country's school districts, Negroes could not count on controlling the schools their children attended; that is what being a minority means. And if decentralization overcame the deadening inertia encountered by any major innovation in the public school system, Jencks argued it would only lead to a provocative brand of parental "interference" with faculty and administration. A decentralized public school would face the same state legislative limitations, curricular and other, that the existing systems must deal with. "Local control," Jencks concluded, "is, therefore, likely to enrage the professional educators, work against the ambitions and hopes of the integration-minded black and white parents, yet end up leaving black nationalists as angry as ever."

The attempt to graft private school initiatives onto the public school system has not succeeded and probably cannot succeed. The tissues are incompatible; Donald A. Erickson, Professor of Education at the University of Chicago, has complained that in the public schools "to a lamentable extent it is *illegal* to school children for adulthood in any but the most staid and conventional ways," and has denounced the school system as an example of those large public institutions that have become "tired, bureaucratic and corrupt. . . .At that point they must be supplemented or supplanted by new institutions, which will hopefully respond more sensitively to the needs of their clients." In this mood some educators are turning their thoughts to private schools with resignation rather than enthusiasm.

Yet there would be reasons to favor the continued expansion of private systems even if the public schools were not going down for the third time under their own dead weight. Consider the example of American blacks. Jencks points out that private black schools provide a constructive channel for the energies of ghetto blacks; only blacks can do this particular job, and its challenge has already contributed to the ghetto a store of organizational and motivational talent that would otherwise have been lost or perhaps expended on violent self-help. The challenge of the founders becomes as well a challenge to the students; their outposts are cities on a hill. The excitement of innovation, of pioneering, animates the black private schools. It is hard to imagine how a majoritarian public system could evoke the enthusiasm of the beleaguered but suddenly successful minority to be seen at Harlem Prep and elsewhere; black literature and school uniforms are all of a piece. Recent well publicized research (the Coleman report) indicates that such an outlook—a student's sense of control of his own future —may be more important to academic success than all the paraphernalia of the best equipped high school.

Private black schools in time may mitigate what *Brown* v. *Board* perhaps in the short run aggravated: black alienation from and bitterness towards white society, which is initially encountered in the public schools. Although black schools will mean, at least initially, black separatism, by that very token they may bring blacks through the cultural "identity crisis" currently facing them. So, at least, argue both Donald Erickson and Christopher Jencks.

Jencks advances the analogy of the Catholic immigrants of the nineteenth century. Like blacks now, Catholic children were offered a public school system oriented around Protestant white middle-class values. Catholic parents did not want the outlook of their children diluted or submerged by those values, and particularly did not want them to return from school ashamed of their own religion and heritage. And like blacks today, Catholics felt that public schools did not provide proper discipline. Jencks also observes that Catholics could not work through the public school system because most neighborhoods did not have so dominant a Catholic majority; blacks now face the same problem. (Some, of course, still believe strongly enough in integration to continue to work through public schools, just as there were Catholics, particularly Italians, who felt that theology had no place in public schools and allied themselves with the Protestant majority.) When parochial schools were being started on a large scale, many feared they would preach racial hatred or separatism, but after one hundred years there is no reason to believe they have fanned intolerance. A defensive minority, Catholic or black, bolsters its confidence and effectiveness by turning to schools that are its own in the most literal proprietary sense.

The successes of the private black schools of New York, Chicago, and Boston indicate that the turn to them, a reaction too spontaneous to be called a decision, was correct. Separatism is a way for blacks to achieve for themselves some of the educational goals the public school system hardly even aspires to for them. By maintaining a sense of black identity, which public schools may like to squelch, blacks are trying to achieve academic ends, just as by guarding *their* identity Quakers formerly sought to advance their spiritual ends. In both cases the goals seem incompatible with public education, which is by definition majoritarian and by nature inimical to the survival of enclaves. It is the proudest boast of America's public schools that they supplied the heat under the melting pot.

A human being needs more than programmed instruction

and well-lit classrooms to excel. He needs not only a goal, but also some idea that his own efforts can get him there. Educational parks and other projected public school nirvanas will deny in TV-filled classrooms what blacks have been able to give themselves in storefronts: a mission and a calling, to use the suddenly apropos evangelical bywords. Those Americans who have lost or outgrown their own have something to learn from Harlem Prep.

⊙⊙⊙⊙⊙⊙

# CHAPTER FIVE

# Voluntary Justice

ON MONDAY THE TWELFTH OF MAY, SIX HUNDRED AND eighty- three years ago, William of Lawford abandoned hope of settling his quarrel with Reginald of Northampton. William and Reginald were merchants who had fallen out over the sale of a horse at the famous fair of St. Ives, England. They had decided on a price of five marks for William's horse, and also apparently agreed that Reginald could pay with goods, not surprising since specie was often hard to come by in the Middle Ages. Reginald then had given William a bolt of ray, valuable shiny cloth. Immediately the deal was chilled, for Reginald, having no doubt that the cloth was worth five marks, demanded his new horse, while William indignantly denied the ray could possibly bring that sum and refused to hand over the steed.

Thereby, in 1287, appeared all the elements that have classically paved the way for a commercial lawsuit—disgruntled seller, unhappy buyer, disagreement over the value of goods. But these men did not hie away to the closest King's judge. Merchants like William of Lawford and Reginald of Northampton took advantage of a private court, the Fair Court of St. Ives. There they carried their dispute, and there it was speedily settled by townspeople and other merchants like themselves. The "citizens, burghers, and merchants" of St. Ives appraised the cloth at only two marks. Reginald could not produce the other three, so he did not get his horse. Furthermore, the appraisers found that the horse was worth merely three marks. That meant William would have come out two marks ahead if he had sold it for five, so he was awarded the cloth as well as the horse, to give him the value of his abortive bargain, something lawyers would take another few hundred years to analyze and name a party's "expectation."

All this went on in a "court" that was purely voluntary, in fact, extralegal; neither King nor Parliament imposed the rules it followed or enforced the decisions it made. Wherever merchants regularly gathered, a few among their number were selected to resolve their quarrels, and a booth set apart at the crowded dusty fair to which disputants could, if they wished, have recourse. The courts moved with the merchants, and consequently earned the appellation "piepowder," or dusty-footed.

Sovereign unto themselves, these merchant courts settled most of the important trading disputes of England and of much of Europe for several hundred years, completely outside the framework of the common law. And they also from time to time adjusted questions that had little or nothing to do with commerce. When Maud Ledman accused Thomas Barber of "using vile words against her" and "taking her by the shoulder and throwing her into a certain well," she resorted to the same Fair Court of St. Ives that had looked after William of Lawford's horse trade the year before.

It is a little surprising to find so much important litigation being handled in this fashion. Compulsion—the persuasive knock of the sheriff—could be called upon to enforce only the decisions of the country's official courts, and so one would expect people to use those courts when they could not come to terms between themselves. The merchants' courts were voluntary, and if a man ignored their judgment, he could not be sent to jail. If the loser disagreed with a Fair Court's decision, he could theoretically take his case into an official court and start over from the beginning. Nevertheless, it is apparent that Fair Court decisions were generally respected even by the losers;

otherwise people would never have used them in the first place. "The hand-clasp is mightier than the fist," the American Arbitration Association asserts, and the sentiment may well make up in truth what it lacks in literary elegance.

Merchants made their courts work simply by agreeing to abide by the results. The merchant who broke the understanding would not be sent to jail, to be sure, but neither would he long continue to be a merchant, for the compliance exacted by his fellows, and their power over his goods, proved if anything more effective than physical coercion. Take John of Homing, who made his living marketing wholesale quantities of fish. When John sold a lot of herring on the representation that it conformed to a three-barrel sample, but which, his fellow merchants found, was actually mixed with "sticklebacks and putrid herring," he made good the deficiency on pain of economic ostracism.

The system worked. In the volumes of legal artifacts meticulously edited under the sponsorship of the Selden Society, scores of representative cases decided over a period of several hundred years are reported. Merchants became a law unto themselves.

The complete circumvention of official courts, one of the oldest and best established of civilized institutions, and the voluntary forfeiture of what would seem to be the most fundamental and essential characteristic of any court—the ability to enforce its judgments with legal coercion—present interesting questions about just what it is people want in the way of justice. Scholars have devoted a great many hours and a great many pages to investigating the Fair Courts' success, and the beginning of the answer, at least, is self-evident: medieval merchants must have considered their interests better served by voluntary submission of disputes to one of their own number than by formal common-law actions. Fair Courts had obvious advantages of speed and economy, especially to men who in a few weeks would be returning to their homes perhaps a thousand miles away or moving on to another of the great European fairs.

Equally important was the way in which merchant courts went about making their decisions. Consider again William of Lawford's horse trade. The whole case turned on how much the horse was worth and how much the cloth was worth. The court appointed expert appraisers to make the determination on the spot; no such simple resolution could be had at common law. The more technical the issue, the greater the advantage of having it worked out by those in the trade rather than by outside judges.

Official courts were hamstrung by rules that made them particularly unappealing to merchants. Such courts, for instance, would not handle disputes involving contracts made overseas, an impossible situation which led to the custom of claiming that various foreign towns were located in English shires. If a trader made a deal in Honfleur, France, he might solemnly allege that the transaction occurred in Honfleur in the County of Kent, England; the judge went along with the fiction or deprived the trader of a remedy. If the agreement provided for interest, no matter how low, official courts regarded it as usurious. Or suppose the man being sued claimed he had already paid and brought in his books of account to show the debit. Common-law courts would not even look at such evidence, though among merchants it had high standing.

Today men condescendingly smile at the idiosyncrasies of the common law as merely another side of the benighted Middle Ages. But common-law judges did not think themselves peculiar or archaic. Quite the contrary, they could congratulate themselves and their predecessors on the great progress of the law since Anglo-Saxon days, when a trial consisted merely of a general oath-swearing called a compurgation; if enough people denied a debt was due, it was not due, period. That kind of procedure had little appeal for practically anyone, so the official Anglo-Saxon courts were virtually ignored, and voluntary arbitration became the customary mode of settling disputes long before the Norman Conquest.

By comparison, medieval procedure could pride itself on rationality and progressiveness. But it simply did not change as fast or act as fast as commerce required. Voluntary courts, on the other hand, could accommodate their procedure to the needs of the moment and the desires of their patrons. In official courts, changing a particular rule or adapting a particular reform only substituted a new rigidity for the old and meant that the next day another rule and another reform would have to be equally laboriously wrought out. The rules had to apply to everyone, and too many interests had to be satisfied simultaneously in a sovereign's courts for them to satisfy any particular interest very well. Justice should be blind, but that handicap seriously limits its efficiency. Affording protection needed in one in a hundred cases means incurring cost, inconvenience, and delay in the other ninety-nine.

Take, for example, the hearsay rule. This principle excluded merchants' account books from evidence for hundreds of years in common-law courts, although the common-sense Fair Courts always allowed such records to be used. In modern times, common-law courts finally began to accept business entries in evidence as an exception to the hearsay rule, but the original practice has not yet been so cleanly exorcised from the law that judges can ignore it. Exceptions to old rules become new rules which make courtrooms only that much more arcane. Consequently businessmen are still avoiding courtrooms when they can.

Whether because of the courts' inertia or expense or unfairness or complexity, for practically as long as there is legal history there is a parallel history of recourse to voluntary extralegal forums to settle disputes. There, on the basis of their own private requirements, the parties can make their own law and their own procedure directly, rather than mediately, through the legislature. They can avoid the expense of procedural protection they do not need, and the inconvenience of laws they do not like. So in Athens five and a half centuries before the birth of Christ arbitration was favored; Maimonides urged it on his followers; George Washington insisted in his will that any disagreements about it were not to be taken into court, but were to be submitted to three impartial men, who were to make their decisions "unfettered by law or legal construction" solely on the basis of what they thought the writer's intentions had actually been.

And so today a far greater volume of disputes than most people realize are settled by voluntary private "courts," probably many more than are actually litigated. The Fair Courts of the Middle Ages have their successor in the arbitration process resorted to daily by businessmen of every description. The impetus behind this development strikingly recalls just the problems that led to analogous results six and seven hundred years ago.

The modern history of arbitration begins with the American Civil War. With the blockade of the South, a great many contracts involving the purchase, delivery, and resale of cotton were thwarted. Ships became unavailable or were sunk trying to run the blockade. Prices leaped and tumbled unpredictably. Neutrality and contraband-of-war laws introduced further complications. Insurance policies, if obtainable at all, carried complex provisions that had to be reinterpreted to determine their application to every new contingency. The sum of it all was a swamp of contract claims the courts would have taken years to untangle, and then perhaps not resolved consistently or to the general satisfaction of the trade.

Voluntarily united in the Liverpool Cotton Association, the merchants of Liverpool who handled the great bulk of the trade agreed to insert an arbitration clause in all their contracts, avoiding the necessity of resort to the courts for settling the inevitable disputes. Arbitration proved so successful in adjusting differences without the expense, inconvenience, and hard feeling of suits that other Liverpool commercial associations took up the device, first the Corn Trade Association and then the General Brokers Association.

The movement spread to London very shortly. First the great staple dealers—corn, oil seed, cotton, coffee—then the stock dealers and produce merchants, and finally professional associations of architects, engineers, estate agents, and even auctioneers adopted the practice of regularly inserting an arbitration clause in every contract to which they were a party, guaranteeing that the transaction, however sour it went, would never see a court.

By 1883 a correspondent of the London *Times* could write that "whole trades and professions have virtually turned their back" on the courts, a remarkable national transformation to have occurred in only twenty years. Once the "private courts" were tried, their advantages quickly became apparent, and the London mercantile community, which only a few years before had been making tentative inquiries about Liverpool's experience with arbitration, now found itself the object of an American investigation.

Samuel Rosenbaum, who made the study, reported back to the Philadelphia Bar Society that a commercial case in a law court was a thing of the past in England. He found European arbitration, which was merely a compulsory first step in the judicial process, relatively unsuccessful; in England arbitration worked, he concluded, because it was voluntary, entirely extragovernmental right down to the critical question of who would be the judge. Arbitrators handled thousands of cases a year, and the practice was gradually spreading out from the trade associations that had initially popularized it.

Glowing reports such as Rosenbaum's helped arbitration expand in the United States around the turn of the century. The practice was already familiar, but relatively unexploited: the New York Chamber of Commerce had been appointing arbitration commissioners at every monthly meeting for over a hundred years. Throughout the nineteenth century, however, official courts played the major role in the settlement of commercial disputes. Only from the early 1900's did arbitration begin to attain substantial popularity in this country, but by the end of World War I it had become the preferred practice in many lines of business.

Before 1920, nowhere in the United States could an arbitrator's award be taken into court and enforced; the remedies available to an American merchant in such a case remained about the same as those of William of Lawford in 1287. Yet it was in those same years before 1920 that arbitration caught on and developed a following in the American mercantile community. Its popularity, gained at a time when abiding by an agreement to arbitrate had to be as voluntary as the agreement itself, casts doubt on whether legal coercion was an essential adjunct to the settlement of most disputes. Cases of refusal to abide by an arbiter's award were rare; one founder of the American Arbitration Association could not recall a single example. Like their medieval forerunners, merchants in the Americas did not have to rely on any sanctions other than those they could collectively impose on each other. One who refused to pay up might find access to his association's arbitral tribunal cut off in the future, or his name released to the membership of his trade association; these penalties were far more fearsome than the cost of the award with which he disagreed. Voluntary and private adjudications were voluntarily and privately adhered to, if not out of honor, out of the self-interest of businessmen who knew that the arbitral mode of dispute settlement would cease to be available to them very quickly if they ignored an award.

One of the major American propagandists for arbitration, Owen D. Young, comparing the experience of Europe (which enforced arbitral awards in the courts) with America (which did not), concluded that the most compelling sanction was not legal, nor even economic, but the private moral censure to which a violator would be subjected. That sounds wildly, almost laughably, utopian, but it came not from a philosopher but from a Chamber of Commerce man who was interested in the best way to get things done.

Now legislation has formalized what had long been the norm: binding settlements. An arbitrator's award is enforceable in court in all fifty states, and twenty-four have a uniform statute under which a court will automatically carry out the award unless whoever is objecting to it can show that it is fraudulent. From the campaigns of fifty years ago arbitration has grown to proportions that make the courts a secondary recourse in many areas and completely superfluous in others. The ancient fear of the courts that arbitration would "oust" them of their jurisdiction has been fulfilled with a vengeance the common-law judges probably never anticipated. Insurance companies adjust over fifty thousand claims a year among themselves through arbitraton, and the American Arbitration Association (AAA), with headquarters in New York and twenty-five regional offices across the country, last year conducted over twenty-two thousand arbitrations. Its twenty-three thousand associates available to serve as arbitrators may outnumber the total number of judicial personnel—federal, state and local—in the United States, but certainly exceed by many times the number of federal judges. Add to this the unknown number of individuals who arbitrate disputes within particular industries or in particular localities, without formal AAA affiliation, and the quantitatively secondary role of official courts begins to be apparent. Marx would presumably be pleased to note that, judicially, the new state, or rather nonstate, has already taken root in the vitals of the old, grown up, and largely supplanted it. Among businessmen, official courts have been displaced by private agencies as a means of settling the majority of day-to-day disagreements.

The judicial system of the political state is now in competition with another system devised by merchants, suggested Wesley A. Sturges over forty years ago. Now peaceful and even symbiotic coexistence has replaced competition. The "political state" itself occasionally prefers private arbitration to its own judicial system: the AAA is often called upon to conduct union representation elections under the National Labor Relations Act, and it has even been enlisted by the Office of Economic Opportunity to supervise the selection of poor peoples' representatives, whom Congress wished to be members of antipoverty agencies at the local level. The proposed postal legislation discussed in Chapter Two yields a more far-reaching point. Certain labor disputes between the Postal Corporation and its employees, if not resolved within the organization, would be referred to the American Arbitration Association for final settlement. If enacted, the government in many cases involving contract interpretation would be voluntarily denying itself the use of its own courts.

The courts themselves display a friendly disposition towards arbitration. English judges used to be less benign. *Scott* v. *Avery,* the case that in 1856 set a precedent for judicial enforcement of agreements to arbitrate, explained the judges' prior antipathy in very basic terms. "As they had no fixed salary, there was great competition to get as much as possible of litigation into Westminster Hall, and a great scramble in Westminster Hall for the division of the spoil." The more cases that went to arbitration, the fewer fees that went to judges. Today, by contrast, the last problem in the world likely to be facing any court is a shortage of cases.

In New York in the 1920's, when the idea of arbitration was rapidly catching on, twenty-seven thousand cases clogged the state courts' calendars, and it took five years for a case to come to trial, with no prospect of early determination even then; one celebrated case had been in progress for thirteen years. For all practical purposes, the system of governmental judicial administration had broken down, except for a litigant with unlimited funds and patience. In some large cities today the problem remains as bad, or worse; courts are too overburdened to cope

with their job, except with great delay. The tradition of arbitration, on the other hand, has always been speed, ever since medieval merchants required that complaints be answered in an
hour or a day and that final decisions be handed down by the
third tide. In New York today, it may take four and one-half
years to come to trial in a routine automobile accident case;
arbitration can be completed in four to eight weeks. It is not too
much to say that official courts can function, even as slowly as
they do, because of the breathing space permitted them by arbitration. If every legal dispute went to court, the logjam might
sink the judiciary altogether, so it is more than willing to see
arbitrators getting a bigger and bigger share of its business.

"This upward movement," recounts an enthusiast, "has
been distinctively by businessmen, and not by statesmen, legislators, or lawyers." So it has always been: William Langland's
Piers Plowman in the fifteenth century boasted of his competence as an arbitrator though "in canon or in decretal I cannot
read a line." That is to say, he was altogether ignorant of the
law. To American businessmen, who have held fixed opinions
about the undesirable characteristics of lawyers ever since
colonial times, the arbitrator's nonlegal expertise may be his
greatest recommendation.

In avoiding judges, people who turn to arbitration of necessity escape the law itself, for a man who knows no law cannot
be expected to hand down a decision in comformity with it. In
other words, the system of extralegal, voluntary courts has progressed hand in hand with a body of private law; the rules of
the state are circumvented by the same process that circum-
vents the forums established for the settlement of disputes
over those rules.

During the 1930's, when political scientists and politicians
sought new worlds for government to conquer, the widening
domain of arbitration began to strike some commentators as
anomalous, and even dangerous. The intellectual climate did
not favor private judicial preserves, and critics for the first
time began to recognize the profoundly antistatist implications
of arbitration. A lone Canadian writer, noting that Hitler's
accession had stayed the growth of arbitration in Germany,
saw a larger lesson: "For the totalitarian state, with its doctrine
of the all-enslaving power of the state . . . arbitration means an

attempt by private individuals to free an important part of their activities from the dominating yoke of the governing group." That argument, however, did not appeal to several American observers, who believed that official encouragement of extralegal dispute settlements was an abdication of the state's prerogatives at a time when they should be expanded.

The feeling against arbitration merged with the prevalent distrust of other manifestations of private enterprise. A Harvard Law School student warned that "it is untimely to cast aside this socialized orderly process [of official courts] for the laissez faire individualism of lay arbitration." In context it is apparent that "laissez faire individualism" is pejorative, and a socialized process is held up as the ideal.

A good deal of insight accompanied the antipathy of such skeptics, for they recognized and commented on aspects of arbitration that had hardly even occurred to its original proponents, particularly its silent displacement of not only the judiciary but even the legislature. With horror the critics concluded that in arbitration the law was simply abandoned. Consider, for instance, the very common rule that in breach-of-contract cases the aggrieved party can collect only the losses he actually suffers or a reasonable advance estimate of them (liquidated damages). If a pepper dealer contracts with a merchant to pay damages plus a penalty of two percent, the merchant cannot collect the penalty in court—the agreement to pay it is against the law. But if the contract contains an arbitration clause, an arbitrator can (and in an actual case did) assess the "illegal" two percent penalty. In short, a private agreement between two people, a bilateral "law," has supplanted the official law. The writ of the sovereign has ceased to run, and for it is substituted a rule tacitly or explicitly agreed to by the parties.

"Law," however, presumably binds all the people all the time. If an arbitrator can choose to ignore a penal damage rule or the statute of limitations applicable to the claim before him (and it is generally conceded that he has that power), arbitration can be viewed as a practically revolutionary instrument for self-liberation from the law, "incompatible with general concepts of positive law," Professor Henrich Kronstein distressfully observed: the phenomenon challenged his whole view of the legal order. No theory, he concluded, can obscure the essential lawlessnesss of this form of "private government."

Now the theoretical issue brought to light for the first time by Depression-era statists has become largely moot, for modern codes often specify that individual parties may vary the codes' provisions by agreement, thereby bestowing the imprimatur of the state upon "laws" privately agreed to by particular businessmen or companies. Just as official courts have welcomed the relief afforded by the private alternatives, official statute-framers have gladly accommodated their handiwork to the undeniable fact of private law. More than that, the lawmakers have recognized that the specificity of a privately negotiated contract term or "law" is superior to a rule that by its very definition must be universally applicable, and hence cannot discriminate among particular needs and particular occasions. The Uniform Commercial Code, a widely adopted set of laws pertaining to commercial transactions, favors the private alternative by allowing businessmen both to pick the set of laws that will govern their dealing (whether of Michigan or New Mexico, for example, when a buyer lives in Michigan and a seller in New Mexico) and to vary particular Code provisions by agreement. Neither option would have been available at common law; legislatures now, by contrast, actually move over to make way for their person-to-person, voluntary substitutes, saving for themselves only the power to prevent outright fraud or bad faith.

Merchants have always been among the first to feel the necessity for private courts, but arbitration has never confined itself solely to commercial disputes. To return again to the Fair Court of St. Ives, the reports tell how Roger Barber undertook for nine pence to cure John, son of John of Eltisley, of baldness. John mustered enough enthusiasm for his anticipated repilation to pay Roger in advance. Roger wrapped him up in a plaster for a Tuesday and Wednesday in 1288, and, as the record laconically states, "withdrew from the vill." A chastened and still bald John sought the aid of the merchant court.

Roger Barber probably saw no good reason to submit himself to the jurisdiction of a voluntary tribunal for the obvious reason that he had little to lose by absenting himself. That hard fact has trammeled the growth of private courts outside a business context. Nevertheless, more and more noncommercial quarrels are finding their way to the arbitrator. Separation agreements, for instance, now almost routinely provide for arbitration of disputes arising over the custody and visitation rights of the respective spouses.

Noncommercial arbitration has received its most extensive application in Philadelphia, where all claims for under two thousand dollars must be arbitrated before they can be taken to court. Members of the Philadelphia bar sit on panels to hear these small claims; thus the system operates in accordance with the substantive law rather than outside it, although sessions are quite informal. It also differs from conventional arbitration in that it is nonvoluntary and an appeal is available to the courts. The Philadelphia system was instituted to take some of the pressure off the Municipal Court, and it succeeded in reducing delays there from two years or more to five months. From the improvement it is obvious that a great many complaints that formerly had to be dealt with judicially are now finally resolved by arbitration, and the figures bear out this conclusion: in 1958, of 5,740 arbitrated cases only 190 were appealed. That small percentage does not necessarily demonstrate complete acquiescence in the results in the other 5,550 cases; some claims are far too small to be worth the cost of taking an appeal to court. In fact, in some such cases, occasionally referred to by the bar as "dog-bite cases," arbitration provides a remedy where no economically feasible way of recovery previously existed. It is fair to conclude that the small number of appeals does reflect reasonable satisfaction with the way arbitration works in practice, and the Philadelphia program therefore provides some evidence that arbitration can succeed outside the ambit of the trade associations, which originally nurtured it.

Victims of automobile accidents, who today make up a major portion of almost any local court's workload, have traditionally eschewed arbitration because in court their damages could be assessed by a jury presumed to be sympathetic, or at least susceptible to the eloquence of counsel: such a jury might award many times the actual money or "special" damages to an injured driver in order to compensate him for pain and suffering and other intangibles. This attitude is not unfounded; it appears that in arbitrations under New York's uninsured motorist statute, damages are often limited to the "specials." On the other hand, in Philadelphia one investigator has found that a plaintiff appears to have a statistically better chance of recovery by arbitration than before a jury. Indeed, some talented defense lawyers ask nothing better than a jury, feeling that the common sense of the laymen may save their client in situations where a judge's fascination with new concepts of liability grounded in attenuated legal subtleties might, financially, hang the same client.

If it is safe to generalize from both the Philadelphia and the New York experience, it may be that juries return fewer but larger verdicts than could be had from an arbitrator.

Individuals may increasingly resort to arbitration for the same reasons that have made businessmen and corporations such firm supporters of extralegal courts: economy, speed, privacy, and expertise. Cumulatively, such advantages may well come to count for more than the possibility—it is only a possibility—of a very large jury award. If an automobile accident victim wants a jury in a major metropolitan area, it can mean a delay of, literally, years before his case even comes to trial. A trial will last for days and sometimes weeks, incurring legal expenses that can amount to a substantial fraction of the recovery, routinely one-quarter to one-third, and sometimes one-half. If technical questions are involved, litigants must take the chance that the judge and jury may not understand their explanation of them. Hours can be consumed in out-of-court maneuvering, and in the coutroom itself, legal conventions such as evidentiary rules sometimes seem to impede rather than to forward the cause of justice. And while a party may by that time not much care, he will more often than not come out of the suit with one or more lifelong enemies.

He may also, to be sure, come out with a great deal of money, a scandalously great deal, in the opinion of some. But in many cases it can hardly be worth the time and effort; whether or not justice is done, the price may be just too high and the chance of failure too great.

The Accident Claims Tribunal of the American Arbitration

Association has already amassed experience and expertise in handling the routine tort claims, which remain the greatest stronghold of the courts. The sheer unmanageability of the volume of auto accident cases provides ground for a prediction that more and more of these disputes will ultimately find their way before an arbitrator.

The complexity of the legal process may succeed in driving private individuals to arbitration even if the courts' caseload does not. Suing one's neighbor is, initially, a fairly simple operation, one of the simplest known to the law. Hobert Greedy engages a lawyer, explains his problem, and probably pays him a retainer. Hobert's lawyer then draws up a complaint, a formal legal document stating the grounds on which the jurisdiction of the court rests and in practice reciting in considerable detail, often for several legal-size pages, what happened and what Hobert wants his neighbor to do about it. A number of copies of this document are prepared, along with "certificates of service" to be returned to Hobert's lawyer as evidence that Hobert's neighbor has indeed received the complaint. When the papers have gone from Hobert's lawyer through the Clerk of Court to the sheriff to the neighbor and back again, the suit is officially commenced, with as few papers and as few lawyer-hours and as little complexity as almost any process known to the law.

With this, now contrast the method for initiating an arbitration under a contract that specifies that means of settling disputes arising under it. The complaining party need not consult a lawyer if he does not want to; he can take a printed form out of his desk drawer (such as the AAA form here illustrated) and describe in his own words what his grievance is. The paper is then mailed to the other party, and a copy deposited along with the contract at the regional office of the American Arbitration Association. That commences the arbitration, at the cost of five minutes and a few postage stamps.

## AMERICAN ARBITRATION ASSOCIATION, Administrator

Commercial Arbitration Rules

### DEMAND FOR ARBITRATION

DATE:

TO: (Name) ........................................................................................
(of party upon whom the Demand is made)

(Address) ........................................................................................

(City and State) ........................................................................................

Named claimant, a Party to an Arbitration Agreement contained in a written contract, dated
which agreement provides as follows:                    (Quote Arbitration Clause)

.hereby demands arbitration thereunder.

NATURE OF DISPUTE:

CLAIM OR RELIEF SOUGHT: (amount if any)

HEARING LOCALE REQUESTED: (City and State)

You are hereby notified that copies of our Arbitration Agreement and of this Demand are being filed with the American Arbitration Association at its ....................................
Regional Office, with the request that it commence the administration of the arbitration. Under Section 7 of the Commercial Arbitration Rules, you may file an answering statement within seven days after notice from the Administrator.

Signed..................................................................................
(May be Signed by Attorney)

Name of Claimant..................................................................................

Address..................................................................................

City and State..................................................................................

Telephone..................................................................................

Two copies of this Demand and the Arbitration Agreement must be filed, and the administrative fee paid, as provided in Section 47 of the Rules, in order to institute proceedings.

FORM C-2 AAA 6M 12-68 INTEGRITY

# Form Used to Initiate Arbitration Under AAA Rules

The process for bringing an argument before a private court is, then, infinitely more speedy and economical than that for bringing an identical dispute before an official court. Why not, one might wonder, simply reform the official procedure to bring it into line with the private methodology? That superficially sensible idea, however, is not helpful and not even really plausible. An official court, armed with the whole power of the state, including the power to bring an unwilling party before it, evict him from his home, and sell it out from under him to satisfy the court's judgments, has to have its powers circumscribed with the most elaborate and punctilious procedures to be tolerated. These niceties have evolved over hundreds of years to guarantee, for instance, that a man will not be subjected to this kind of power without notice of what is about to happen—hence the elaborate complaint, service of it, and notice of service returned to the initiator of the action. But whatever the historical, theoretical, and practical reasons for the painstaking, measured pace of the courts, that pace also entails an abundance of two increasingly expensive commodities, paper and lawyers. A private court, on the other hand, is the voluntarily constituted tribunal of the men who stand before it. Some of the safeguards appropriate in a different context— rules of evidence, to mention one—are not necessary there.

The expenses, delays, and sometimes even injustices of official courts are the inevitable concomitant of their ultimate reliance on force. Such reliance is necessary only in an extremely small percentage of the arguments to which men have always fallen prey. For almost all the others, voluntary private courts provide a superior alternative, so superior that the state's monopoly on dispensing justice, as old as Solomon, is in reality no longer a monopoly at all, but a residual power over particularly intractable cases.

ⓞⓞⓞⓞⓞⓞ

# CHAPTER SIX

# Protection Money

IN NEW YORK CITY, THE EIGHTY-SECOND PRECINCT
Station House is in Harlem on West 135th Street between Seventh and Eighth Avenues. All night every night a patrolman
covers the block, protecting beauty shops, stationery stores and
groceries from the burglaries that formerly plagued them—six
in two weeks before the patrolman began his regular rounds.
Fifteen merchants rely primarily on him to prevent a recur-
rence of the robberies.

The patrolman's vigilance costs the merchants $2.25 an
hour, not because they are periodically shaken down, but because he has no connection with the Eighty-second Precinct
Station House; the Leroy V. George company supplies his services. Private policemen can be hired in most large American
cities and are being hired with increasing frequency as their
public counterparts become less able to give the protection city
residents need. Joseph Valdez, a barber on West 135th Street,
chairs the association of businessmen on his block who turned
to the Leroy V. George Agency when the Precinct Station House
there failed to intimidate any burglars.

Private protective services are not the sole prerogative of

Harlem shopkeepers, nor of businessmen in general. On the other side of the country, the "Bel Air Patrol" guards the residential sections of Bel Air, California, whenever it is engaged to do so; the Patrol belongs to magnate Howard Hughes, a one-time resident of Bel Air, and he leases the Patrol's services to his former neighbors.

Private police have not come recently on the American scene, and they are not the only, nor necessarily the most important, example of free enterprise protection services. But they most graphically exemplify dissatisfaction with public efforts at crime prevention and the agility of entrepreneurs at capitalizing on such dissatisfaction, even next door to a police station, as on 135th Street. Every deterrent device from sentry dogs to electronic alarm systems is enjoying an economic boom. Some are even being franchised, the ultimate stamp of apple pie mainstream Americanism. While it may be many years before rent-a-policeman stands crowd the streets as ubiquitously as McDonaldburger arches, the total private expenditure on law enforcement already exceeds half of the amount of money spent on public police at all levels of government. The President's Commission on Law Enforcement and the Administration of Justice calculated that public police services cost Americans about $2.79 billion a year, while they pay $1.35 billion for various private prevention services and another $200 million for a miscellany of protection equipment, bringing private expenditures to 56 percent of public outlays.

Why are some people paying a billion and a half dollars a year for police protection other people assume comes free? An obvious explanation would be the inadequacy of publicly provided services, and this factor no doubt goes far towards accounting for the phenomenon. Alan Adelson reported a case history of a single block in the Bronx for the *Wall Street Journal:* As slums have crept up on all sides of the once prosperous neighborhood, its elderly inhabitants' homes, populated by the remnant of a characteristic exodus to suburbia, have become a battening ground for criminals and addicts. Adelson discovered that hardly a household on the block had escaped burglary, robbery or assault some time in the last two years, and as a result its residents are now prisoners in their own homes. No one willingly ventures onto the streets after late afternoon, apartments are barricaded like miniature fortresses, and many of the area's old men and women keep arms close at hand. The burden of fear in these people's lives is more than economic: simple conveniences like home delivery of dry cleaning are no longer possible because householders will not unbolt their doors for any unfamiliar face, and evening strolls through the streets are no longer a form of recreation. Even a dedicated barbershopper had to give up his nights with his group because of the danger of the trip home.

Naturally enough, people surviving from day to day in fear of their bodily safety have begun to attempt to supplement New York City's police protection. City police are not, by and large, considered very useful; a robbery victim recounted that after the intruder left he called the police emergency number only to be quizzed about details while the robber sat in a cab at the corner waiting for a green light to make good his escape. One building has organized its own miniature police force; tenants take turns standing guard in the lobby, sometimes equipped with dog and walkie-talkie. But the fearful more often resort to a new burglar-alarm company, practically the only thriving business enterprise in the neighborhood. According to Adelson's story, proprietor Jerome Neth's door-to-door salesmen sold eight $350 alarm systems the first week the store opened, and Neth aims for a force of two hundred salesmen to service the area. Enough burglar-alarm sales at $350 apiece for the commissions to support two hundred salesmen in one Bronx neighborhood mean multitudes of burglar alarms; it is apparent these people are for all practical purposes supplying a good part of their own police protection. Efforts like theirs across the country account for the Law Enforcement Commission's previously quoted statistics.

Individual efforts at self-protection do not resemble traditional police services as closely as the organized patrols that have appeared in some cities. Of these, the best known is the Jewish Defense League (JDL) in New York City. With a claimed membership of six thousand and chapters in New York City, Philadelphia, Cleveland, Montreal and Toronto, the JDL enjoys its reputation as an independent private police force, and copes with the notoriety of a private army. Last summer it ran a newspaper advertisement picturing an armed youth, captioned, "Is This Any Way For a Nice Jewish Boy to Behave?" Its nice Jewish boys regularly patrol three neighborhoods in Brooklyn and one on the Lower East Side. The League appears to be financed primarily by voluntary contributions rather than by the actual sale of its services, so it does not really qualify as a free enterprise police force, though it certainly performs police functions. Jewish shopkeepers in Passaic, New Jersey, called on the JDL for help in August 1969, when a riot approached their area, and over a dozen members, armed with shotguns, immediately responded. (The riot did not get close enough to test the League's effectiveness as a deterrent.) Led by Rabbi Meir Kahane, the organization is convinced that public police can't or won't do enough to keep slum-area thugs from systematically and violently preying on Jewish merchants and residents, so it attempts to fill the breach with its own members.

But critics complain that the JDL takes the law into its own hands. On a smaller scale, similar groups have appeared across the country, often being stigmatized as vigilantes and no doubt in some cases crossing the line between legal self-protection and illegal intimidation. Nobody objects to harbor patrols by boat owners alarmed by the rising number of boat thefts when the vigilantes are armed only with bourbon and peanut butter sandwiches. But different nuances of the same concept of voluntary self-protection can create considerable alarm. In Redding, California, six men instituted a nightly car patrol, only to earn the choler of the mayor along with the gratitude of the police. Back on the East Coast, Mayor Hugh Addonizio of Newark has attacked Councilman Anthony Imperiale's "North Ward Citizens Committee" as a threat to the public safety. The Committee claims five thousand members and uses forty shortwave radio-equipped automobiles to patrol the streets of strife-ridden Newark.

In Cairo, Illinois, opposition to a two-hundred-man force, known as "White Hats" after their riot helmets, focused on its alleged antiblack orientation; the group disbanded early in the summer of 1969 pursuant to a suggestion from the state's attorney general. Unfortunately, in more than one case the bad judgment of patrol leaders in undertaking activities of questionable legality has limited their value. No instance is more regrettable than that of the Black Panthers, who only a few years ago were a small ghetto patrol organization. In an ironic reversal of the usual situation, the Panthers contended not with inadequate police protection, but with the police themselves: blacks wanted protection from the state monopoly that was supposed to protect them. *Quis custodiet custodes?* is not a question that went out with Latin. Panthers supplied "guards for the guards" by following police patrol cars through black districts and "monitoring" any arrests that were made. Since the Panthers were armed with shotguns (legally), it may well be believed that their mere peaceful presence tended to discourage idle harassment. Private black police, like private black schools, contributed to the drive, élan and self-sufficiency that suffer whenever the state has exclusive control over a necessity; a Negro remarked, "I think it's beautiful that we finally got an organization that don't walk around singing." The Panthers have now gone national and become involved in more controversial projects, but so far as can be determined, their original patrols were entirely salutary, even if the Panthers were as racist as the "White Hats."

The various citizens' patrols serve as a substitute for one particular type of police activity: the deterrence of nonprofessional crimes in metropolitan areas against the persons and property of individuals and small businessmen. While this area by no means exhausts the responsibilities of public police, it has proved (whether because of manpower, financial, or other limitations) one of the most difficult for them to cope with. In short, private police have tackled the most intransigent, not the easiest, protection problems, and have succeeded—when they have succeeded—where their public counterparts have either failed or simply not been able to take on the job.

For an example of a private police force organized on a full-time basis and performing across almost the whole spectrum of normal police activity, one must leave the patrols. The most elaborate and best institutionalized of all the full-time forces are the railway police, maintained by many lines to prevent pilferage from cars, thievery from passengers, embezzlement by employees, or other illegal activities. Jeremiah P. Shalloo's study of private police for the American Academy of Political and Social Science, though now over thirty years old, has not been superseded, and the picture he presents of railway police organization remains the closest thing we have to a prototype for a complete and autonomous private police force. At the time he conducted his investigation, more than ten thousand men earning at least eighteen million dollars a year were employed full time as railroad police.

The modern history of the railroad police dates from general reorganization at the end of World War I and the founding of the Protective Section of the American Railway Association. Railway police compiled a remarkable record of effectiveness: between then and 1929 they succeeded so well that freight claim payments for robberies decreased 92.7 percent, from $12,-726,947 to $704,267. With the onslaught of the Depression and, consequently, greater inducements to pilferage, the figure began to rise again, though without detracting from the luster of the previous decade's accomplishment. Statistically, arrests by railroad police have resulted in a higher percentage of convictions than those by their municipal counterparts. A five-year sample from the Pennsylvania Railroad showed an 83.4 percent conviction rate, while a thirteen-year sample from another line revealed a conviction rate of 97.47 percent, although the record may have been assisted by a now declining facet of free enterprise law enforcement, Justices of the Peace who are paid on a fee basis.

Railroad police, armed with .38 caliber revolvers, are entitled by statute to exercise normal police powers. Within their domain they may arrest any violator of the public peace, not just offenders against railroad property. One court has held that in "making arrests for violation of law not immediately concerning property of a railroad company, [railway police] officers act not as agents of the company, but as municipal policemen." In short, they stand as a sterling example of privately recruited, trained, and paid law enforcement officials.

That distressed Shalloo. Railroad police reminded him of the Middle Ages. "They are modern private armies," he wrote. "The fact that so few complaints have been directed against them is eloquent of the efficiency with which they are controlled by the railroads. In Pennsylvania the state exercises no control whatever over these police. It simply meets its contractual obligations and after conferring police power forgets all about it. Railroad police are responsible to the company by which they are employed and paid, and to no one else."

The activities of railroad police have not in modern times given any cause for fearing that private performance of such functions will lead to serious abuses, particularly when the standard of comparison is the conduct of public police. Shalloo's reference to the railway police's widespread reputation for good character and high ability poignantly contrasts with the present status of many big-city public forces; sanctions against misconduct are so ineffective or roundabout that they may as well not exist, however rhetorically comforting the forces' status as servants of the people may be.

When there is opposition to private policing activities, it ostensibly rests on their supposed lawlessness, their proclivity for taking the law in their own hands. Yet in most cases their activities are perfectly legal, and sometimes are even authorized by a state statute. New York, for instance, has an elaborate organic provision for railway police, granting them all the powers of policemen in cities and villages for the arrest of persons who commit offenses on property under the railroad's custody. The law requires railway police to undergo certain tests, and is careful to note that "compensation. . . shall be such as may be agreed upon between [the policemen] and the corporation" (that is, no public money is to be used). Authorizations such as this statute exist in various states for a wide variety of organizations, including "camp-meeting societies." In each case, "public" powers are conveyed to policemen recruited, supervised, and paid by private societies.

The so-called vigilantes can often operate on no less sound legal ground. The *Wall Street Journal* survey that unearthed several of the previously noted groups observed that only last summer did Illinois repeal an 1885 statute permitting voluntary law enforcement associations, while in New Jersey Governor Richard Hughes twice attempted and twice failed to get legislation that would spell the end of the North Ward Citizens Committee. The Redding, California, group also conducted its patrols within the letter of the law.

Pennsylvania is unusual in having two general private police statutes, one applicable only to Philadelphia and the second to other towns. The laws allow municipal mayors or courts

to grant privately organized and employed patrolmen or watch-
men the power to make arrests and to carry arms in the same
fashion as public police officers. These provisions spell out very
clearly that no public money is to be spent on such patrolmen,
so it is clear that they contemplate a completely private supplement to municipal police protection, recruited and paid for by
individual householders. Probably many states have similar
laws, for they are really nothing more than an updated version
of the familiar concept of the *ad hoc* sheriff's deputy, a private
citizen enlisted to meet the emergency of the moment. But
large cities' dangerous streets require continuous surveillance,
and that fact calls for the present-day variation on the traditional theme. Bank robbery and cattle rustling were discrete
events that necessitated enrolling a posse of deputies for only
a few hours or a few days.

No modern figures have come to hand, but in 1933 there
were 304 private patrolmen with police powers in the city of
Philadelphia alone, each paid according to his own contract
with the individuals and businesses whose district he watched.
The law has not been changed in the interim.

In the face of the indisputable legality of most private protection services, commentators persist in frowning on them.
The frightened reaction of many officials to perfectly legal
efforts at self-protection by people—black and white—whose
neighbors are patently not being protected by the police suggests that antipathy to "vigilantism" is not the same as antipathy to lawlessness. The conviction grows that the groups' mere
existence is more offensive than their alleged lawlessness is. As
they do for other enterprises—the post office, the courts, and
the schools—some people harbor a deep if unconsidered belief
that protection should be a government monopoly. Shalloo
summarized his own feelings on the subject at the outset of his
work: he felt "convinced that private police are [although pres-
ently indispensable] a legal anomaly, a constitutional contra-
diction. The term 'police,' connoting as it must delegation of
power from the State or a creature of the State, implies a public
character, just as 'army' and 'judge' connote public or State
derivation."

The soundness of that logic may be tested by examining the
simile on which it rests. If police naturally partake of "public-

ness" because armies and judges do, the case for exclusively public police rests on very shaky ground. Judges, as the preceding chapter emphasized, are being supplanted by private arbitrators more and more often. (Even "private armies," the ultimate epithet cast at nonpublic police, ought to strike a responsive chord somewhere in most Americans. The "shores of Tripoli," celebrated in the "Marine Hymn," were fought on by a total of eight Marines, assisted by a private mercenary army made up of some two hundred fifty Greeks, rebellious Arabs, and Bedouin camel cavalry, recruited by an American civilian named William Eaton. It wasn't much of an army, but it did the job at a time when Congress would not.)

The prejudice against private police can at least claim a respectable pedigree, and moreover one that began on streets no safer than today's. The continuous indiscriminate crime in parts of New York, like the section of the Bronx described earlier, resembles nothing so much as eighteenth-century London, with the craving for narcotics replacing gin as the stimulus to much of the violence. London produced its own version of private police: the Bow Street Runners, the ancestor of all modern police, whatever their genre. Their patron was no less a personage than Henry Fielding. Everything about the experiment combined to convince Fielding that the work could be better done by the government, although his operatives were clearly superior to none at all. The novelist, in his capacity as London magistrate, recruited several reliable individuals; the little corps became known as the Bow Street Runners from the location of Fielding's office and earned renown for its exploits as a free enterprise thief-taking service, financed on a per capita basis by public or private rewards. But Fielding continuously agitated for governmental financial assistance so his platoon could be regularly salaried instead of dependent on erratic payments for services. He drew up a blueprint in 1753 for a police force that anticipated in many respects Robert Peel's "Bobbies" of seventy-six years later.

For all its disadvantages, the Bow Street Runners greatly improved upon other contemporary free enterprise law enforcement operations. Then as now there were corrupt policemen: Fielding's *Jonathan Wild* recounted the career of an all too unfictional thief-taker who made a successful business out of identifying robbers and retrieving stolen goods. Wild, unfortunately, would as soon accept business from a thief as from his victim, and was ultimately hanged for working both sides of the fence too egregiously.

Englishmen opposed on principle the very idea of public police during Fielding's lifetime. They feared the relation between police and what is known now as the police state. A historian of Fielding's career as a magistrate observed that Englishmen preferred to rely for protection on the "normal human desire for looking after one's own interests." (A system of "common informers," men who received a portion of the fine when prosecutions they helped launch were successful, survived in England until 1951.) Eighteenth-century Britons resolutely believed private enterprise was the most efficient way of capturing criminals.

The inadequacy of free enterprise law enforcement, brilliantly publicized by Henry Fielding, became and remained a part of Anglo-American collective wisdom, taken for granted by people who never heard of Jonathan Wild or who think he leads a rock group. The assumption, reenforced in the United States by half-remembered stories of Judge Roy Bean ("the law West of the Pecos") and hemp-happy vigilantes, in some cases became a conviction that public police should exclude, and not just supplement, their private predecessors. Fielding's campaign ultimately resulted in a brand of intellectual overkill, which hampers rational consideration of today's alternatives.

The objection that railroad police, or any private police, usurp the functions of the state presupposes that protection is or should rightly be a state monopoly. Most people, not least the railroads, see it as a state *responsibility*. But when the responsibility is not completely discharged—and can it ever be?— everyone from railroads to householders should remain free to take up the slack with his own resources, which he could not do if protection were made a true governmental monopoly. Nothing would suit the residents of that declining neighborhood in the Bronx better than to save their $350 per apartment burglar-alarm costs, or the residents of Newark better than to have official patrol cars on the streets of the number, frequency and effectiveness of Anthony Imperiale's, or the Baltimore and Ohio Railroad better than to have special government detectives assigned to protect its more valuable shipments.

Even, however, if public police could consistently discharge all their responsibilities in a manner that satisfied their constituency, one would not wish summarily to terminate private law enforcement in the United States, for it enjoys its own efficiencies, not unrelated to those exploited by other competitors with would-be government monopolies. When an individual pays directly for his protection (instead of indirectly through taxes), he is careful not to buy anything he does not need, and has the power to make sure his police spend their time providing the kind of service he wants most. A man who wants protection will fire patrolmen who waste their time harassing minorities or who waste time in any other way. No private policeman has ever spent many hours at a restroom peephole in hopes of apprehending deviates. Instead, he protects the special interests of his client, and in the process may (as railroad police did) develop an expertise not realistically within the grasp of public forces.

On a different plane, eighteenth-century England may not have been so very wrong when it postulated private greed could more effectively protect individuals and enforce the laws than a state agency. That stimulus differs from individual law enforcement efforts motivated by brute fear, but both motives work together: witness the burglar-alarm companies and patrolman-supply companies mentioned earlier. There are people whose answer is to move into an environment where police protection will be less vital, such as the virtual strategic hamlets going up around Washington, D.C. These adjuncts to municipal services have been examined from the standpoint of the person who needs protection; attention may now be turned to an examination of the problem from the perspective of the individuals doing the protecting.

In the courts themselves, the American legal system increasingly relies on private suits to implement laws that have nothing to do with personal safety. Such suits represent, functionally, a modern renaissance of the ancient *qui tam* action, whereby a person sued in behalf of the state and kept part of the fine. The oldest and best known American examples of this kind of private enforcement activity are antitrust treble damage suits, in which a company that is injured by another company's violation of the antitrust laws may go into court and recover three times the damages it actually suffered. The provision for treble damages makes the remedy very much like a penal fine imposed in a criminal action brought by the state, but the "fine" benefits the person who prosecutes the offender, not the state. Of course, if there has been an antitrust violation, the government can, and usually will, prosecute on its own, but commentators tend to agree that the real teeth of the law, the sanction which more than any other keeps businessmen honest when approaching the boundaries of antitrust legality, is the private treble damage suit. Private suits also play a large role in enforcing the securities laws, even when there has been no prior government prosecution.

The obituary of the *Gentleman's Magazine* in 1746 for Colonel Sir Thomas de Veil, Henry Fielding's immediate predecessor as Bow Street magistrate, with only slight modifications could be applied to a good many antitrust and securities-law plaintiffs today: "Upon the whole, he seems to have been a remarkable instance of how far vices themselves may, with respect to the public, supply the want of private virtue." Without unimaginable increases in money devoted to public enforcement, it is doubtful that some of the laws nearest to the heart of the American economy could be executed, otherwise than sporadically, in the absence of auxiliary private suits, which make the risks of violation not worth the possible gains. The dynamic of self-interest, dollars and cents (but mainly dollars) self-interest, is already more important to law enforcement than most people realize. If this enforcement energy could be expanded beyond merely economic crimes to assaults on person and property, the results might be remarkable.

In Michigan, about fifteen years ago, at least one local government engaged a private profit-making company, Charles Services, Inc., of Kalamazoo, to patrol its streets and apprehend traffic-law violators. Charles Services' patrolmen wore a typical police-style uniform, with the corporation's own crest emblazoned on the arm. It seems that the company assisted in bringing the speeders it caught to trial, and it offered its traffic-patrol services for at least three and a half years under a contract that compensated it by the hour. The patrolmen, who were made deputy sheriffs to protect the legality of the arrangement, were averaging sixty hours a month for the town that employed them.

One of the advantages of the arrangement was that Charles Services' patrolmen could be put on at peak traffic hours and released during slow periods; employing them by the hour may have been more economical than adding more men to the local police force.

It was the opinion of the corporation's president that his men had to hew the line more carefully than official policemen, since they did not enjoy civil service status or a political term in office, the comforting shield and stanchion of bureaucrats. All in all, the idea seemed to work well and is more intriguing today, in light of the personnel difficulties from which practically every major metropolitan police force apparently suffers, than it was in 1955.

The police contract eventually found its way into court by a route so oblique that the legality of the arrangement was not actually at issue. A conviction obtained after an arrest by Charles Services' police was upheld on technical grounds, with a hint that the patrolmen's status as deputy sheriffs was enough to empower them to enforce the laws. A dissenting judge, however, slashed out at the whole arrangement with such ferocity that it was subsequently abandoned. Charles Services is still in existence, but no longer does contract police work.

The judge who administered the *coup de grace* was offended that anyone should make a profit out of law enforcement, and apparently did not consider it relevant that a profit-making company might do the job more cheaply than a non-profit-making sheriff. The profits on sixty hours a month of traffic patrolling must have been modest, but more than distaste for profit inspired the judge's dissent. He believed as an article of political faith that the state and its subsidiaries should play the sole role in protecting its citizens.

That is a creed boasting ancient antecedents and resting on a deep belief in the primacy of public over private interests, if not on skepticism about even the existence of an autonomous private interest in the area of protection. Horace summarized the philosophy in an epigram, *Nam tua res agitur, paries cum proximus ardet.* The metaphor is persuasive; when your neighbor's house is burning down, your own is endangered. Protection is everybody's concern and therefore properly the state's monopoly, to abbreviate the now familiar syllogism. The difficulties with a *laissez faire* approach to fire protection may not have been precisely what inspired Horace, but it certainly reenforces his thought.

However, as a matter of fact, there are free enterprise fire companies in Grants Pass, Oregon; Billings, Montana; Nashville and Knoxville, Tennessee; Rochester, New York; and Scottsdale, Arizona. They put out fires for their paying customers.

When a customer's property is endangered, they put out nonsubscribers' fires, too, for common-sense reasons. The Rural/Metropolitan Fire Protection Company of Scottsdale (formerly just the Rural Fire Protection Company but now dousing wider horizons) is also happy to put out fires even when they do not endanger a subscriber's home, for business and not eleemosynary reasons. Unless the victim tells the company he would rather his house burned, it is legally entitled to assume he wants the fire out, extinguish it, and collect the "fair value" of its services from the non-subscriber. The Arizona Corporation Commission has held that "fair value" may be calculated as seventeen times the annual subscription rate, so long as the company actually does the victim some good and does not just wet down the ashes of a total burnout. That final proviso supplies an incentive unusual in the field: nothing saved, no pay.

For all these reasons, the specter of Rome burning while the firemen fiddle because no one in Rome will pay unless everyone pays—which in one form or another supplies the major rationale for government dominance of the whole protection field—is false and empty. No fewer fires need be extinguished by a private voluntary service than would be by a municipal monopoly.

Problems of coverage are not, in any event, unique to private departments. R/MFP, far from being the product of a campaign against government monopolization, was conceived by an individual who lived just outside the city limits of Phoenix and had the unsettling experience of watching neighbors' houses burn down while the Phoenix department stood by to keep the sparks that drifted over the city line under control. President, Fire Chief, Treasurer, majority stockholder and Lord High Everything Else ("You might say I've got a fairly firm grip on the outfit") Lou Witzeman moved to a suburb of Phoenix in 1947 and discovered that he had no fire protection, and that the only way he could get any was to organize a fire company. He quit his job as a $60-a-week reporter specializing in conflagrations and other city news, and set about collecting $10 apiece from a thousand committed neighbors, learning, he says, "one of the greatest lessons of my life: my neighbors were a bunch of lying S.O.B.'s." Eighty percent decided they didn't want fire protection after all when it came time to pay for it. So Witzeman contacted several thousand more to raise his initial ten thousand dollars.

The operation quickly progressed from one truck and four men to one truck and two men as Chief Witzeman matched its size to its resources. But now, twenty-two years later, the company operates thirty-seven trucks out of nine stations with forty full-time firemen and another hundred who can be called when needed. It makes a remarkable claim: it provides top-quality around-the-clock fire protection for its customers with the most effective equipment in the industry at a cost per person served that is about *one-fifth* the national average for fire departments.

The corporation works under contracts with its customers, who in some cases are private individuals and in others are municipalities. Scottsdale, with a population of 70,000, is the biggest; it pays its bill on a lump sum basis, monthly, just as a large corporation might pay an insurance premium. In Green Valley, Arizona, the Rural/Metropolitan Fire Protection Company provides police and ambulance service as well as fire protection.

Chief Witzeman is making out fine, a great deal better than most fire chiefs, but he costs his customers less because his salary is divided among all the communities the company serves. The company pays taxes, buys license plates, pays property tax on its stations, and coughs up corporate income tax as well, while charging householders only twenty percent of the average per capita costs of public American fire departments.

An instinct for survival—something a public department

never has to worry about—has enabled R/MFP to achieve these economies. For one thing, it can spend whatever it considers expedient on research and development, a luxury not granted politically managed departments, since taxpayers are understandably leery about financing anything but men, machines, and water. In the fall of 1969 Witzeman spoke to the National Fire Protection Association in Denver about some of his innovations: a ton-and-a-half truck converted into a mini-fire engine that is faster, lighter, more maneuverable and much, much cheaper to run than the red monsters; radio-controlled beepers on off-duty officer's belts; a fire truck with two pumps, one of which can either be used in tandem with the other or be dropped as an independently powered unit wherever needed.

The company is also quick to spot and employ useful ideas from other sources, such as a chemical which reduces the friction drag on water running through long hoses, and a German fitting which allows any number of lines to branch off a large supply line, each with its own individually controlled water-pressure regulator.

On the other hand, R/MFP is not so quick to buy brand new, super shiny, goliath fire engines. It has no developing-nation-showpiece-investment, Aswan-dam complex. It builds some of its machines and obtains others used; the flagship is a hook-and-ladder hand-me-down from Los Angeles. Sometimes towns stumble along with reverse priorities: not a dollar for Research & Development but the biggest, reddest water thrower west of Dubuque. When, however, the boss's salary depends on his efficiency, a company can develop a marvelous knack for distinguishing what people need badly enough to pay for, from what they merely think would be nice. Witzeman's perceptivity on the subject has been continuously honed ever since he couldn't collect those ten-dollar bills in 1947.

The chief, treasurer, and principal stockholder of R/MFP did not begin with any feelings on the desirability of municipally owned versus private fire protection service. But his company's greatest obstacle has proved to be other people's preconceptions on the subject. Because of the assumption that fire fighting is the government's job, the corporation doesn't "fit into anybody's rule book." It puts out fires, perhaps better and certainly more cheaply than its public cousins. But because nobody ever heard of a privately owned fire department, what should be routine management problems become major challenges. Insurance companies and banks look askance at this intruder into the sovereign domain. It is different, and, Witzeman laments, "in this IBM, punch-card civilization of ours, that makes us suspect." This subtle cost of public monopolization came closer to derailing the enterprise than any other single factor. Since R/MFP could not be accommodated with a carbon copy, it could not be accommodated at all.

Witzeman persevered, with an illogic that is the special strength of the entrepreneur. If he had known anything in the beginning about either fire fighting or accounting, he would have realized he was bankrupt from the start, and retreated as graciously as possible. Not being burdened with the lugubrious facts, he went ahead and made money. All the dozens of useful crackpots whose harebrained schemes have been chronicled in these pages shared this blindness to reality, which is a pejorative synonym for progress. Harnessed to it is their own mad energy, which no public enterprise can exploit, and which, in fact, is rarely even called into being except in some independent endeavor.

If, however, on *a priori* grounds, private enterprises are assumed to be foreclosed from a field, the field will lose the *élan vital* that has recurred in so many forms. Assumptions as well as laws can snuff the flame. There is nothing to keep other individuals from emulating Witzeman's example except the attitude that was Rural/Metropolitan's own nearly fatal nemesis.

◎◎◎◎◎◎

# CHAPTER SEVEN

# Paying for Roads

HENRY CLAY ONCE SUCCINCTLY EXPLAINED WHY HE favored giving the federal government responsibility for building roads. His argument has been complicated but not fundamentally changed in our own times. It is, Clay said, "very possible that the capitalist who should invest his money in [turnpikes] might not be reimbursed three percent annually upon it; and yet society, in its various forms, might actually reap fifteen or twenty percent. The benefit resulting from a turnpike road made by private associations is divided between the capitalist who receives his toll, the land through which it passes and which is augmented in its value, and the commodities whose value is enhanced by the diminished expense of transportation." From "society's" point of view, capital should be put into roads unless some other investment yields more than twenty percent, but Clay's hypothetical investor loses interest in roads whenever something else yields more than three percent. Such an investor will never put the optimal amount of money into roads, because he can demand tolls only of actual road users, not of local landowners, farmers and others who benefit from improved transportation. Some economists call this phenomenon "neighborhood effects"—the inability of an investor to recoup from all those who are benefitted by his investment—and it would seem to have particular application to roads, since the advantages of efficient communication ultimately accrue to so many people.

The "three percent annually" mentioned by Clay as a return to investors was no imaginary figure; at the time he spoke the country teemed with investors in private roads who would have been happy to receive a regular three percent dividend on their stock, and observers counted the company that paid that much unusually prosperous. Two or two and one-half percent probably would have been a more representative figure for the companies that did not leave their investors with a completely empty bag. Turnpikes, as the private roads were called from the turnstiles that barred their entrance to unpaying travellers, were bad business by any normal standards.

If "society in its various forms" receives a return of fifteen or twenty percent from investment in roads, but capitalists can extract only three percent by charging tolls, too little money will be invested in roads. Therefore it seemed logical to Henry Clay to have society itself make the investment, through the government. That logic, plus the demands of the travelling public, has carried the day so successfully that the country's road system has today become a *de facto* public monopoly.

Exactly the opposite situation prevailed for most of the important roads of the nineteenth century. From 1800 to 1830 private investment poured into thousands of miles of turnpikes in the United States, notwithstanding the minuscule return the capital earned, and hundreds of turnpike companies built the roads that carried the rivers of emigration to the old Northwest and the products of the newly settled states back to the seaboard. For the first third of the century, constructing the roads that were the only means of transportation to and communication with most parts of the West remained a function of private capital. An occasional exception, like the famous National Road going west from Cumberland, Maryland, was a deviation from the norm.

The history of the grandfather of all the turnpike companies, the Philadelphia and Lancaster Turnpike Corporation, chartered in 1792, has much in common with all the rest. Penn-

sylvania had no desire on principle to commit its program of
road building to private enterprise, and in fact had resorted,
unsuccessfully, to several other expedients before chartering
its first turnpike company. That was the pattern in most of the
states where the companies later flourished; in the late 1700's,
the states tried lotteries, forced road service from local landowners, grants-in-aid to localities, and even offers of large acre-
ages to contractors if they would build roads to the interior. All
these measures failed, as well as the routine expedient of levying taxes and spending them on the highways of the states.
None of the states' financing schemes could begin to supply the
volume of capital necessary for the improvements the people
were more and more vociferously demanding as they in ever
larger numbers pushed to the West. An economist might have
told the states that if the people needed roads that badly, it
ought to be a simple matter to levy sufficient taxes to pay for
them, but then as now political reality was not always condu-
cive to economic models, particularly when the people using
the roads were often using them to leave the states. In view of
the durable consensus on the necessity of publicly financed
roads that developed well before the end of the nineteenth
century, it is a little ironic that the private road companies
should have been chartered only because it proved impossible
for the states themselves to raise enough capital to build the
roads everyone seemed to want.

There was no shortage of takers for the Philadelphia and
Lancaster's stock. Capitalized at $300,000, it arranged to sell six
hundred of its thousand $300 shares in Philadelphia and the
remainder in Lancaster. In the Philadelphia terminus, 2,276
citizens contended for the honor of purchasing the shares allotted to their city, and the six hundred selected by lot to receive
one share apiece considered themselves fortunate. In this respect, the experience of the Philadelphia and Lancaster was
far from typical; many companies succeeded in obtaining
charters from the legislature but never sold enough stock to
justify beginning construction. Nevertheless, the total amount
of capital the American turnpike companies of the nineteenth
century were able to raise and put into roads is astonishing.
They sold their stock at a time before British and other overseas
investors had taken to plunging heavily in America's trans-

portation enterprises, and had to extract the money $50 or $100 at a time from farmers and merchants who had a little money set aside but no interest in professional investments. Most such individuals would take only one or two shares, and the trend in share-pricing reflects the market for the stock; the three hundred dollars a share price of the Philadelphia and Lancaster was soon succeeded by a norm of $50 or $100 a share, and even at the lower prices almost no one bought large blocks of turnpike stock.

None of the companies was capitalized at more than a few hundred thousand dollars; long stretches of road, requiring a million or more dollars for improvement to turnpike standards, were divided up among a number of connecting companies. Small companies and widespread stock ownership were the only realistic way enough capital could be raised to make major improvements in the wretched transportation facilities available in the states after the Revolution. The fragmentation was able to accomplish what nothing else could: building a system of trunk roads, some hundreds of miles long, which linked all the principal entrepots of the eastern seaboard with the watershed of the Ohio River valley.

That was what the turnpike companies collectively accomplished, despite their chronically poor returns, and their seemingly impossibly limited resources. What they lacked in size they made up in number. Dozens upon dozens of companies entered the business before the railroad era sapped its vitality, and in some places corporations continued to be chartered into the 1870's and 1880's. Eighty-four companies had been incorporated in Pennsylvania by 1821, and they completed construction of 1,807 of the 2,521 miles of pike allotted them; at the peak of the movement, 2,400 miles of turnpike were in operation in Pennsylvania alone. New York beat even those statistics, with sixty-seven companies by 1807, one hundred thirty-five by 1811, and fully two hundred seventy-eight different companies, operating 4,000 of their 6,000 miles of authorized road, in 1821.

These thousands of miles of private roads were the best roads America had enjoyed up to that time, and the principal arteries for the movement of both goods and people throughout the period of the first great westward surge. As Henry Clay intimated, they may not have made their owners rich, but from the standpoint of transportation they certainly cannot be faulted, at least not in comparison with any realistic alternatives. For despite complaints about undermaintenance, they were often, by the standards of the era, superlative roads, eighteen to twenty-two feet wide, graded with a rise in the center to facilitate drainage, rarely permitting inclines of more than three or four degrees, and generally surfaced with gravel or broken stone to a depth of a foot or more. Such a road could cost $10,000 a mile to build, perhaps not an intimidating figure to a country now accustomed almost as a matter of course to spend a million dollars a mile on its superhighways, but one which represented the mobilization of capital on a scale theretofore unprecedented in the United States. The Philadelphia and Lancaster is said to have spent, all told, $465,000 on constructing its road (or more properly, improving it, for like most turnpikes, it was built along an older trail), an average of $7,500 a mile. The result was accounted a masterpiece of the engineer's art and, more to the point, a boon to the thousands of Conestogas that coursed its length.

The Valley Turnpike in Virginia was still considered an outstanding example of road construction in 1900, sixty-five years after the company was chartered. During the Civil War it stood up under some unusual traffic—railroad engines hauled along it between nonconnecting spurs by teams of forty to sixty horses. In the twentieth century it introduced a revolutionary engineering innovation to American road building, asphalt surfacing, a technique which soon became commonplace. All the Pike's reputation, however, did not make it profitable, and under the company's last president, Harry F. Byrd, its shareholders conveyed the road to the state in 1918. No one ever made any money on the Valley Turnpike, and the characteristically low return to most road company shareholders has already been mentioned.

It is at first surprising that the companies attracted as many investors as they did, and that the investors kept on pouring money into the roads when no profit could be hoped for; an example is the Valley Pike's post-1900 investment in bituminous surfacing. The explanation for this seemingly irrational investor behavior perhaps lies in the interests of the people who bought the stock. No systematic analysis has been undertaken, but it appears that stockholders and perhaps officers, too, were precisely the people who Henry Clay thought were benefitting from roads without paying for them: local merchants and property owners. The University of Virginia Library preserves an 1839 broadside issued by the Valley Turnpike Company to counties that had not met their stock "quotas"; apparently the cost of building the road was distributed fairly precisely along its stretch. Everyone who enjoyed a turnpike's so-called external economies paid for them by giving it the use of his money at little or no interest. No doubt an occasional dreamer hoped to profit on the stock *per se*, but speculators would probably have dealt in larger than the one- and two-share lots in which most turnpike stock moved, and they would probably have gotten cold feet long before the end of the turnpike movement. In large part, America's first passable network of roads was probably financed by just the people who stood to benefit from them indirectly, aided by tolls from the people who used them. The durability of the turnpike era may be explained by its underlying economic rationality. But naturally the stockholders welcomed the chance to turn the onerous burden of continual maintenance over to the state as soon as the state would assume the responsibility. Then they could have their roads for free, they thought.

The "turnpike era" of American history is generally said to have drawn to a close in the 1840's, when railroads began to replace roads as the primary mode of commercial transportation. A future generation of historians, however, may distinguish another turnpike era in our own times. They might date it from the opening of the Pennsylvania Turnpike in 1940, and will have to extend it at least to the 1970's, for turnpikes are still being built, and once again constitute some of the most important arteries of ground transportation in the United States. The electric eye has replaced the turnstile in many cases, but in other respects today's turnpikes are near cousins of their predecessors a century ago.

In the crucial area of finance, the family resemblance is particularly striking. Modern turnpikes are generally built by "authorities," independent bodies created by a state to finance, construct, and operate the road. Although there are exceptions, for the most part the credit of the state is not committed to the project. A contractor, for instance, can look only to the Ohio Turnpike Authority for payment of his bills; he cannot collect from Ohio. When the Chesapeake Bay Bridge Tunnel Authority recently failed to earn enough money to pay interest on its bonds, Virginia did not rush to the rescue, contrary to the expectations of some people who did not understand the authority's independent status. The authorities, then, resemble a corporation organized for the sole purpose of carrying on the pay-road business—a turnpike company.

Sometimes the authorities may even try to realize a profit on their investment, not for shareholders, but for the sake of making capital available for investment in related facilities. More often, however, authorities are not profit-oriented, and in that respect differ from a free enterprise turnpike company. Yet regardless of whether it wishes to turn a profit, an authority must raise the capital to construct its road, and, since the people who buy its bonds can look only to the authority's revenues (that is, to tolls) for payment of interest and principal on their investment, must plan to make money. No one will buy bonds if the authority looks too public-spirited and not hard-nosed enough. So even in the absence of shareholders, authorities operate according to considerations that govern the operation of any private company. Bond issues have supplanted stock issues as the normal form of capitalization, and certain tax considerations are involved, but apart from that, today's authorities are financial and economic twins of private turnpike companies such as the Philadelphia and Lancaster.

Just how close this kinship is was revealed by some legislative hearings held in Missouri almost twenty years ago, when that state was debating the advisability of constructing a turnpike. The committee did not ponder whether the external economies (the benefits to nonusers) of a limited-access highway spanning the state would, when added to the benefit to actual users of the facility, equal or exceed the turnpike's cost. Instead, it had to consider exactly the same question as did turnpike builders of a century ago: would the tolls be adequate to pay for the road? Although it would be an agency of the state, the authority responsible for the turnpike's construction and operation would differ little from a private company.

At the Missouri hearing, Mr. L. H. Cather, an engineering

consultant, testified that a turnpike could not be financed at all unless there was a solid prospect that user charges, tolls, would pay for it, and he added that the investment bankers who handled turnpike bond issues were pretty shrewd about making that judgment. The financial record of modern turnpikes had been successful enough to induce investors to oversubscribe the Ohio Turnpike's bonds by $300 million the first day they were put on sale. Bonds built turnpikes, and tolls paid off the bonds. "There is," he emphasized, "absolutely no obligation on the part of the taxpayer. It is just like going to the picture show, if you don't want to see the show, you don't have to pay anything."

An investment banker from Kansas City, John Fogarty, reiterated, "It is going to be the prospective purchaser of the bonds, we think, in the long run, who will be the one to say, 'All right, here's the money, go ahead,' or to say, 'It can't be done, we can't give you the money.' "

Since an authority's bonds are not generally backed by the credit of the state that created it, the authority must pay a slightly higher rate than would be necessary if the state itself borrowed the money and built the road. But this additional expense seemed justifiable to the Missouri legislators, for they wanted the turnpike, if built, to be independent and self-liquidating. "I do not think," said one, "the people of Missouri will approve of going into the general revenue to save a small amount of money on the cost of building a road that ought to build itself or not be built."

For all practical purposes, the turnpike would be a business, and would have to operate like any other business. The legislators would not have to worry about "bond buyers putting their money where it isn't pretty safe"—that is, the decision about the feasibility of the road would not rest in their own hands. "Lawyers, bankers, and engineers," it was declared, "are the safest guardians of the public in this proposition."

Given the checkered financial history of the original turnpike companies of the nineteenth century, it may seem odd that the country should return to a functionally identical method of private financing for many of its major roads today, in fact, until the completion of the first highways of the interstate network a few years ago, almost all its completely modern roads. For, as the quotations above abundantly demonstrate, bond financing by turnpike authorities is a method of enlisting private capital, with all the prerogatives of private capital, for the construction of independent, though not private, roads. Economists perhaps find it ironic that the theory of external economies, so convincing in view of the United States' experience with private roads in the nineteenth century, has played so small a part in the construction of so many of our most important roads: if user charges are inadequate to pay for a turnpike, it will not be built, regardless of the magnitude of the external benefits.

Private road financing has come about because of a variety of considerations that Henry Clay's equation could not include. More is involved than the cost of the road, on the one hand, and the benefits it will produce, on the other. An idea of the complexity of the variables can be gained by an examination of the debate that preceded the construction of the Maine Turnpike, the first postwar toll road. Its history is conveniently summarized in a Brookings Institute study by Wilfred Owen and Charles L. Dearing.

Maine desperately needed a new highway to relieve the increasingly serious congestion along old U.S. 1, created by the annual summer influx of vacationers. But the obstacles to any major improvements by the state itself seemed insuperable. U.S. 1 could not be feasibly upgraded without vast expense because of the continuous strip of business properties—restaurants, gas stations, camping and fishing stores—which hemmed it in along almost its entire length. The condemnation costs of a modern road along that route would be astronomical.

An altogether new route, however, would have to contend with the united opposition of all the commercial interests whose existence depended on a steady stream of traffic along U. S. 1. Even assuming the political objections to a new route could be surmounted, there was no way for the state to pay for it. Although only forty-four miles of road were initially involved, Maine's gasoline and automobile license taxes already were among the highest in the country; an increase in the six-cent gas tax might bring little return if it only induced more people to take advantage of neighboring Massachusetts' three-cent levy. The combination of a sparse population and great popularity as a summer vacation spot meant that state-o'-

Mainers were already paying for roads other people used as much as they did. Bond financing was no more feasible than tax increases; the citizens were not about to amend the state constitution in order to build a road for outlanders to ride on, particularly since the immediate economic benefits would all fall to two Maine counties.

All these factors meant that if Maine was to upgrade or bypass U.S. 1, the vacationers who drove on the new road were ultimately going to have to pay for it. An independent authority would have to raise the money for the interim. The Maine Turnpike was accordingly built by an authority and financed by the sale of authority bonds, notwithstanding the vigorous opposition of the federal government's Bureau of Public Roads, which objected to the theory of pay roads. Political reality made that the only way to get a new road. Whatever the merits of Henry Clay and his American System, whatever the magnitude of the external economies, private capital builds turnpikes and is reimbursed by user charges. If it appears tolls from the road will not pay for it, its bonds cannot be sold and it will not be built.

In theory, as Clay explained, not as many roads will be built under such constraints as ought to be. But there are compensating advantages. Removing road construction from the legislature eliminates some of the political skewers that carry their own inefficiencies—for instance, in Maine, the desire of established storekeepers to use roads to keep funnelling traffic past their front doors. An authority road guarantees the "right road in the right place," again because that is the only kind of road that can be privately financed. Say Owen and Dearing, "From experience to date there is no reason to believe that state legislators can be expected to acquire the necessary technical competence and imperviousness to pressure groups required for the construction of a stable and sound system of pricing for highway service."

The cost of collecting tolls may be less than the cost of raising road money by user taxes. Owen and Dearing's study compared the Pennsylvania Turnpike's 3½ percent collection costs with the 4 percent collection costs of gasoline and license taxes. (Experiments have been conducted in Britain with even more efficient collection devices: solid state meters, located near license plates, which can pick up low-voltage impulses from cables buried at intervals under the road. Then the meter can be read periodically and the tolls that have accrued collected in a lump sum.) Tolls also escape the irrationality of user taxes, which bear only a tenuous relation to how much a road is actually used; a man pays the same for his license plates whether he drives 5,000 miles or 15,000 miles a year.

The financial record of turnpike authorities for the most part confirms the skill of investors in backing roads that will pay. Almost all of them have been able to meet payments on their bonds as they fall due. The exceptions can be quickly spotted by skimming financial-column quotations for the various authorities' bonds: the Chicago Skyway, the Chesapeake Bay Bridge Tunnel Authority, and, until recently, the West Virginia Turnpike. Most authorities have done well, and others, like the New Jersey Turnpike Authority, have exceeded their projectors' rosiest expectations.

What difference does it make? Successful or not, the authorities remain public, not private, entities, and so provision of roads remains a state responsibility, an area occupied by the government to the exclusion of individuals. The apparent accuracy of that analysis measures the deceptiveness of some of these verbal polarizations. It is realistic, therefore, to divide in two the job of providing a particular good or service; and most corporations are probably organized to reflect such a division. There is the job of financing, as well as the job of building and operating. When a public monopoly of the service proves impractical or unsatisfactory, private initiatives may attack either task or both. Recall the dichotomy possibly now emerging in secondary education: state finance and private operation. Just the opposite division characterizes the authorities: private finance and public operation. Little more than habit (and the tax laws) stands in the way of opening the other half of the turnpike enterprise—operation—to private companies. The logic of the situation startled a British economist: "But once roads [are] run on user-cost principles, with payments for roads divorced from the system of general taxation, there is no reason why roads should not be provided as a commercial venture."

Turnpikes are run on user-cost principles, and are indeed

divorced from the system of general taxation. We are already the hardest half of the way to private roads, roads which would, no doubt, be regulated like any utility, and which would have to accept all comers on an equal basis like any common carrier, but still private roads. Actually, the authorities are more than halfway, for in seeking private finance they have accepted a private veto over some fundamental aspects of their operation —route and toll questions, for example. The paymaster calls the tune.

For two reasons, however, it is doubtful that anyone will be able to drive on a road run as a completely commercial enterprise any time soon.

First, income on public authority bonds is tax-exempt and they can be sold at a lower rate of interest than normal industrial bonds. Consequently, it is easier to pay for an authority's road than it would be to pay for a private road. The saving does not represent any true economies, since it amounts to a taxpayer subsidy to turnpike authorities. Furthermore, the saving is much smaller than it was at one time, because as states have conceived ever more imaginative ways to trade on their tax exemption and floated more and more tax-exempt bonds through various authorities, the demand for such bonds has been saturated and higher and higher interest has to be paid to sell them. But still a gap remains between public and private interest rates on bonds, and the gap creates practical obstacles to corporate expansion into the operating half of the turnpike business.

Second, the demand for roads which produced the authorities spawned the Interstates as well, and the Interstates have tightened the public monopoly on highways which the turnpikes promised to erode. The pyramid-building politics behind the Interstates provoked indignation. Their cost—nearly twice as much per mile as originally projected—inspired dismay. Citizens have swallowed the bill, wincing and sputtering at the delays and the price, but still swallowing because, blind to the lesson of the authorities, they considered federal finance the only cure. Having built the Interstates, the country has preempted the major trunk highway market, and has reenforced the monopoly by the awesome prodigality with which it has sated the demand. Private investment in roads will be retreating except for particular projects like bridges. Private roads, visible on the horizon to the keen-eyed a decade ago, now seem more visionary than ever. It need not have been so.

ⓞⓞⓞⓞⓞⓞ

# CHAPTER EIGHT

# The Public Interest

OVER THE YEARS THE PUBLICLY ORGANIZED ENTER-
prises discussed in the preceding seven chapters have developed their own cosmology, which, like Ptolemaic astronomy,
tolerably accounts for most of the phenomena it is supposed to
explain. Suspended at the center of this universe is the "public
interest," a *primum mobile* the existence of which has to be
and generally is taken for granted in any discussion of the
government's proper responsibilities. If one assumes the existence of a public interest, defined tautologically as the interest
of all the people considered as a whole rather than the interest
of any particular group of them, there is a beguiling plausibility
to the idea of entrusting its protection to a public agency.

Particular interests, it is asserted, have a knack for making
hay at the expense of society as a whole, and their selfish influence can only be circumvented if the state alone is allowed to
act for the whole public in delivering certain essential services.
Even arbitration has not escaped criticism on this score: its
growth, a skeptic maintains, "should stir those who would place
public interest before private gain." When used to justify governmental monopolies, the argument necessarily carries two

corollaries: the public is an entity tangible and homogenous enough to have an identifiable interest; and that interest differs enough from the private interests, which would otherwise control, to justify a departure from the normal means of providing goods and services in the American economy.

This congeries of suppositions, conveniently named the public interest, is useful, if at all, as a metaphor, and is deceptive even in that capacity. The haziness of this generally inchoate notion can be pierced by looking at private interference with particular governmental monopolies from a vantage point close enough to see what effects such interference has actually produced. In such close perspective, the appealing assumption of a unitary public interest best served by a monopolistic public agency melts away. As an exercise, all the monopolies previously examined herein could be reconsidered in terms of the public interest, which is their justification. How often in fact have people been harmed by competition with the government from private entrepreneurs?

The frequent failure of the stock notion of public interest to work out in practice ought to suggest that something is wrong with the theory, and this book can appropriately conclude with the not so original observation that for all practical purposes *there is no such thing as a public whose interest can be guarded by the legislature through government monopolization of particular sectors of the economy.*

The observation is characterized as unoriginal because it was formally elaborated fifty years ago in one the great classics of American political science, Arthur F. Bentley's *The Process of Government,* which insisted, "Every classification of a population must involve an analysis of the population into groups. It is impossible—at least, for any pending scientific problem— to make a classification so comprehensive and thorough that we can put it forth as 'the' classification of the population." For that reason, Bentley, a prominent progressive, concluded that the Benthamite notion of the greatest good for the greatest number connoted only "what a thinker in some particular atmosphere believes ought to be the law."

Almost any Washington lawyer engaged in practice before one or another of the regulatory agencies charged with the protection of the "public interest" could testify to the validity of Bentley's conclusions in elaborate detail. The decisions a body such as the Civil Aeronautics Board (CAB) must make in particular cases are very narrow—should there be a new transatlantic route? should Pan Am or TWA receive it?—and it takes a prescient man indeed to say that John Q. Public in his role as passenger will be better served by riding to Paris on TWA than on Pan Am. Bentley long ago pointed out that the process of serving the public interest is in reality the process of accommodating the multitude of conflicting interests possessed by an infinitely fractionated public, interests kaleidoscopically shifting and realigning to present a different configuration from month to month, almost from hour to hour, so that if by gift of supernal insight the legislature could momentarily divine the public interest, the knowledge would be useless the next moment. An abstract *a priori* public does not exist, no more for the Post Office Department or any other government monopoly than for the CAB. The Post Office serves businesses, periodical mailers, private correspondents, residents of high density and low density areas, people who mail hundreds of letters a year and people who mail three; the Department also very immediately concerns still other publics, such as its employees and the taxpayers who contribute to its annual deficit. Any man may belong to one or more of these "publics," or, less probably, to none at all.

An elaborate example of the protean guises the public inconveniently insists on assuming may be borrowed from the history of a former government monopoly of half a century ago. From the fall of 1917 until the spring of 1920 the United States Railroad Administration operated all the railroads in the United States. The Railroad Administration's experience exemplifies the semantic error of polarizing public and private interests.

Nationalization, operation of the railroads as a government monopoly for the benefit of the public, led to no great changes (and consequently no great economies) because the idea of the public was a misconceived abstraction. The object of the game, providing as much transportation as possible as efficiently as possible, did not change merely because the transportation was now being provided in the public interest instead of for the railroads' stock and bond holders. The industry—its size, its problems, its purpose—impelled a fairly well defined course of action. As far as possible, such action had been taken throughout 1917 under private control. The greatest miscalculation of the nationalizers lay in thinking they could escape or transcend the mundane fundamentals of railroad transportation by putting the public in charge. Throughout 1918 the Railroad Administration thrashed about attempting to do things better, usually discovering it was doing them worse instead and then reverting to the prenationalization pattern of operation. By the time the dust settled, the railroads were chugging along very much as they had always chugged before. Who controlled them could not change how they had to be run for best results.

The government's program to standardize equipment provides a textbook case of the failure of a watertight theory guaranteeing vast savings through suppressing private economic fiefdoms. Why incur the expense of manufacturing dozens of different products to do the same job when everything could be made the same? Standardization would achieve economies in production. It would permit more rapid turnout of large amounts of essential equipment. It would facilitate operating efficiency by allowing interchange of parts. Smaller stocks would have to be carried. Complications would vanish all along the line from component supply to running repair.

Something more than economics inspired the prophets of standardization, and they aspired to something more than standardization of equipment. Wages, hours, working conditions, classification systems: all must bear a uniform stamp. Their "gospel of efficiency" included as much gospel as efficiency—evangelistic scientism describes their outlook. All America's railroads would be converted to a homogenized, interchangeable, rationalized power tool, operated by the public for the public.

In their minds, standardization *per se* counted for more than the advantages predicated upon it. Faced with a critical shortage of locomotive power early in 1918, Secretary of War McAdoo (who was also serving as Director General of the Railroad Administration) could have achieved the most rapid results by ordering the work to go full speed ahead with the models already in production. Instead, he delayed ordering new locomotives until specifications could be worked out for six standard types, which were expected to suffice for all the roads in the country. Car orders, too, waited on the completion of the scheme. One of the prime arguments for standardization, *the* prime argument given the desperate shortage of equipment that existed when the government took over, was the time it would save in production. Yet applying it as the Railroad Administration did actually cost time. The first cars delivered under the new specifications barely went into service before the war ended. Locomotives, not even ordered until five months after the takeover, fared similarly. McAdoo could have gained speed by postponing standardization, but he preferred a reverse priority. The ideology of public service thus served to thwart its own professed ends.

Having lost several months at the start, the Railroad Administration faced a new problem: what to do with the 1,430 bright shiny new standardized locomotives. The lines would accept them only under crisis conditions. Each railroad was engineered with a different maximum grade, trestle capacity and clearances; in addition it had its own characteristic traffic patterns and requirements. The combination of all these conditions very precisely delineated the kind of locomotive required for the most efficient operation. USRA standard types nowhere nearly covered the nationwide range of requirements, and sometimes fell comically short of adequacy.

Before the government could dispose of its standardized motive power, it had to enter into suits with most of the reluctant railroads chosen to receive it. One peeved official suggested a more direct way out: melt the entire mess of standardized locomotives into one big casting and erect it in Washington as a monument to the handful of men who, forewarned to no avail, rushed ahead and attempted to "foist their theory on the railroads of America."

Standardized wages presented a different face of the same problem: what suited one area simply did not work in another. USRA's Director of Operations mourned their advent because standardized wages made it extremely difficult to shift labor from one part of the country to another; why move from the sleepy South to the hard-pressed Northeast when one could enjoy the same wage in Georgia as in New York? McAdoo prided himself for his fairness in introducing nationwide wage scales, but standardized wages, like standardized locomotives, came at a heavy price.

The railroads themselves held no brief against standardization as such, and it had probably already progressed further in that industry than in most. But two different things were at issue. There was USRA's nearly metaphysical urge to standardize everything, the devil take the hindmost. Then there was standardization as it existed in the industry, described by the President of the Railway Business Association as "not the edict of a potentate or a board of potentates. It comes up from below. It must make its way by general approval. . . ."

This dichotomy—between the practice that works its way up from the bottom and the practice that forces its way down from the top, sanctified with the halo of public interest—can be profitably borne in mind while studying most of USRA's programs. USRA's special competence and, indeed, *raison d'être* lay in the accomplishment of "down from the top" reforms on a nationwide basis, regardless of the private toes trod upon. It could order what had not been done before to be done everywhere immediately. But *why* hadn't the USRA innovations been undertaken before? One answer was that the selfish pursuit of individual interests had precluded innovation and only nationwide unification made it possible. The experience of the United States Railroad Administration suggests a different answer: the measure had not been undertaken before because its disadvantages outweighed its advantages. The moral of the story was that decisions in the industry had to be made on the basis of conditions that the transfer from private to public operation could not in the least affect. In the long run, what had been decided under private control usually was similarly decided under public control.

A whole series of attempted reforms confirm this hypothesis. "Off-line freight offices" had provided a leading example for those who attacked competitive wastes. These were bureaus for the solicitation of freight traffic located away from the railroads proper. USRA abolished them but rapidly discovered they had performed the essential function of providing indispensable advice and information to shippers faced with the immensely complicated freight classifications and tariffs.

Advertising, an industry then in its infancy, already suffered from modern-sounding criticism: the advertising of individual lines was self-cancelling, it cost heavily but added nothing to transportation, it aroused a desire for travel in people when they could best serve the national interest by staying home. Yet even during the war, USRA's elimination of all advertising stirred cabinet-level criticism. Franklin K. Lane, Secretary of Interior, noted that railroad advertising had been one of the principal stimulants to the development of the National Parks and strongly regretted its demise. Very shortly after the Armistice, USRA itself again began advertising to build up its lagging passenger traffic.

If one had to isolate the single most criticized feature of prewar railroad operation, it would probably be the practice of "long hauling." Long hauling means routing freight between two points over unnecessarily long mileage to keep it on the track of a given railway for a greater proportion of the trip than would be the case if it travelled by the most direct route. During the congestion and delays of the fall of 1917, it was alleged that hundreds of thousands of ton-miles of rail transportation were being lost because self-seeking roads practiced the long haul. If the lines were merged into one big system, no one would benefit from the long haul, so it would die unmourned and the public would realize huge savings.

The lines *were* merged into one big system, and several neglected features of the long-belabored long haul soon emerged. In the first place, while virtually all the congestion was in the northeast United States, the long haul existed primarily west of the Mississippi. Theodore H. Price, the Administration's actuary, pridefully listed for the readers of the progressive news magazine *Outlook* some of the long hauls that had been eliminated. Every example he cited is west of the Mississippi, and the most impressive instances involved trips from the West Coast to points in the Midwest, that is, mileage which presented no transportation problem whatsoever in the fall of 1917. Even if USRA's claims for its accomplishments were accepted entirely at face value, 1918 savings from the elimination of the long haul amounted to .002 of the total number of miles travelled, a fraction so minuscule that it lacked any significance.

Furthermore, even that saving may have come at the cost

of less efficient traffic movement caused by overloading the more direct lines when at the same time relatively sinuous ones could have accommodated many more trains. The *New Republic,* already soberer than in the first heady days of nationalization, noticed that the overall economies were "paltry" but stoically predicted great things to come, a remarkable steadfastness in the faith since McAdoo had ordered total unification and the elimination of all long hauls his very first days in office.

Long hauling, a *cause célèbre,* a practice denounced by innumerable authorities for seemingly innumerable years, symbol and exhibit A of the wastes of private operation and self-seeking competition, in the upshot amounted to almost nothing, a microscopic molehill.

If long hauling aroused the greatest prewar indignation at the wastes of private operation, the major wartime publicity fell on executive salaries. McAdoo, in the absence of any major economies, appealed to the public by stressing the part of his program that would eliminate "fancy salaries." No doubt $100,-000 a year did strike many people as exorbitant compensation. Economically, however, the salaries had limited significance when set against total USRA expenditures: McAdoo's well-publicized pruning did save $14.6 million a year, but even this was more a matter of book-juggling than salary reduction, since the executives in question were merely transferred from government to private payrolls. The Director General subsequently discovered that good men came high. He ended by paying his regional directors $40,000 to $50,000 a year. (They served for that only as a contribution to the war effort, and most resigned in the months after the Armistice.) So ended, a victim of economic reality, what in the first half of 1918 was touted as USRA's greatest reform.

Coal zoning (requiring that coal mined in a certain area be marketed there to save transportation), the sailing day plan (holding less than carload shipments for dispatch in a lot on a given day to save on handling), and solid train dispatching all went the way—out—of short-routing and standardization after the Armistice. Nearly every one of the careful plans to save millions of dollars a day, however well conceived, was derailed by some barrier of inexpedience.

A common obstacle afflicted all the well-intentioned improvements: they did not improve. What was already there was there because it served a purpose, even if not readily apparent. "Competitive waste" usually turned out to be another word for service to the shipper or public, service whose value became apparent only when the "waste" was curtailed. (For instance, someone posthumously thought up thirty-seven duties performed by the off-line freight agent.)

The World War I experience is fascinating because brilliant men sat down to calculate all the savings that could possibly be made through an end to competition, nationwide unification, and government monopolization in the interests of the public. They possessed the power to implement their conclusions and ran each of them through the operating mill in 1918. But in 1919 they emerged, with very few exceptions (a major one was consolidated terminals), having rejected the innovations and returned to the prewar pattern of operation. Under the prevailing conditions, the prevailing pattern of operation did not admit any major improvement.

The great expectations of the nationalizers were disappointed at every juncture. How did they go so far wrong in their forecasts? Their objective had been to substitute a rational political control for a capricious economic one, the pursuit of the public interest for the pursuit of private gain. Part of the difficulty was that nonpolitical control proved to be a good deal less capricious and more rational than even its supporters had realized; politicalization could not significantly improve on it. Also, political control turned out to be less than single-mindedly rational: for example, although USRA never developed any problem with corruption, favoritism, or even payroll-padding, a purely political battle between President Wilson and the Republicans in Congress held up a $750 million appropriation whose necessity no one questioned, and thereby detrimentally affected rail transportation for most of 1919.

The underlying misstep that left the nationalizers holding such empty bags was, however, neither overlooking the disadvantages of political control nor encountering a *status quo ante* beyond improvement. Their underlying miscalculation was putting their faith in the substitution of public for private control when no such animal as the public existed. The Railroad

Administration's experience proved the distinction untenable, and on that untenable distinction the nationalizers had raised all their hopes.

In practice, the public reduced to the same passengers, shippers, and officials with whom the railways had always dealt. The long series of futile attempts to save money for the public at large always came at the cost of some element of the public in particular, that is to say, a private interest. The public interest to be served by nationalization did not exist apart from the aggregate of private interests served by the *ancien régime*. The public interest had to be served as it had always been served: in the individual persons of passengers, shippers, and receivers.

Late in the history of USRA the question of just what constituted the protean, elusive "public" became an explicit issue, one which went so deep that it left real rancor in the highest levels of the Democratic Party.

After the Armistice of November 11, 1918, the Wilson Administration became acutely concerned about the adjustment of the economy to a peacetime level of production and a peacetime price level, which everyone assumed would be much lower than the tremendously inflated wartime peak. To supervise and as much as possible to cushion the changeover, President Wilson appointed George N. Peek to head an *ad hoc* commission, the Industrial Board. The Wilson Administration intended to use the government's great war-power leverage on the economy, as exercised through the USRA, the Fuel Administration and other bodies, to direct it to a satisfactory adjustment. At the beginning, no one even thought to examine the implicit assumption of the whole scheme: these agencies, since all served the same "public" and did not serve private interests, would simply choose the best possible course of action. Exactly the opposite happened. No one agreed on what was implied by the "public." The public interest proved a completely unmanageable abstraction. The recommendations of Peek's Industrial Board led to a bitter split in Wilson's cabinet, with both sides cabling the absent world statesman in France to buttress their own interpretation of the public interest.

Controversy over the price of steel rails lit the fuse. Peek and the Board decided the price should be maintained at a high level as part of an overall policy of stemming the anticipated deflation. Walker D. Hines, McAdoo's successor as Director General of Railroads, refused point-blank to purchase rails at what he took to be bloated prices. Peek made a speech including an unkind swipe at Hines as a man "too jealous of his own prerogatives to see beyond the confines of his little czardom" and demanded that he buy rails at the administered price "in the national interest." The government railroad monopoly, in short, ought to be willing to cooperate for the general good, instead of pursuing its private selfish interests. Such a demand from one government officer to another illuminated the fallacy of the whole philosophy of public operation of the railroads in the public interest. *Whose* interest was the public's? USRA's? The Industrial Board's? Did the national interest require expensive commodities or cheap commodities? The wartime Food Administration, officially charged with stimulating production *pro bono publico,* sided with the Industrial Board because high prices would raise output. USRA, no less devoted a custodian of the national interest, naturally wanted cheap rails and so opposed the Board. Since both were government agencies, the confusing semantic issue of public versus private interest was in great measure clarified, or rather dissolved. There was simply no universally comprehensive entity whose interest could be consulted. There were steel mills and railroads in this particular case. Both claimed to defend the nonexistent side of the angels, the public.

The World War I experience of the Railroad Administration does not demonstrate that the millions of discrete individuals who make up the American public have irreconcilably conflicting interests. It may well be that a given course of action will produce more satisfaction, if that can be measured, for more people than any other course of action, and will somehow accommodate the essential needs of most of the people whose lives the problem touches. But that is something very different from merely doing what is right by the "public," conceived unitarily. While there is a theoretical plausibility to public, majoritarian control of an industry or service if one thinks of the public as a discrete indentifiable mass with uniform and homogenous interests, the conceptual appeal breaks down when government monopolies are recognized as the vehicles for a majoritarian stranglehold on institutions that serve an infinite number of constantly shifting minorities. The necessary accommodation of interests may plausibly best be achieved, to use a favorite current shibboleth, by pluralistic institutions. Paul Goodman's criticism of American society in general particularly fits monopolies: "[T]he centralizing style of organization has been pushed so far as to become ineffectual, economically wasteful, humanly stultifying, and ruinous to democracy . . . a situation in which modest, direct, and independent action has become extremely difficult in every field."

The scattered, discursive anecdotes collected here ought to suggest that direct and independent action is still possible, on a scale which is more than modest, even in "naturally" public enterprises. But independent action encroaches on ancient habits, laws, and fiefdoms, which grew up unremarked while generations argued over whether the state should help those who wanted help. The coming generation is already struggling instead over whether the state can step aside when individuals prefer to serve themselves.

(a)(b)(c)(d)(e)(f)

# Bibliography

*Chapter One*

Despite the number of volumes of United States postal history, there is no full-scale study of private postal service in America. But historians of the Post Office provide some information about the private carriers because of the havoc they wreaked on the Post Office. Most of the major express companies carried mail at one time or another, so their historians, too, supply details. One of the earliest in this category is A. L. Stimson, *History of the Express Companies and the Origin of American Railroads* (New York, 1858). A history originally delivered as a speech by one of the movers of the whole development is Henry Wells, *Sketch of the Rise, Progress, and Present Condition of the Express Companies* (Albany, 1864). Alvin F. Harlow, *Old Waybills* (New York, 1934), is the sole source for almost all the material on the California carriers. More recent is Alden Hatch, *American Express: A Century of Service* (New York, 1950). Postal historian Henry M. Konwiser, *Colonial and Revolutionary Posts* (Richmond, 1931), covers the early period.

Further details come from contemporary commentators, led by the irrepressible Lysander Spooner, *The Unconstitutionality of the Laws of Congress Prohibiting Private Mails* (New York, 1844). Albert D. Richardson's *Beyond the Mississippi* could not be found, but was utilized via quotations from it printed in the *Richmond News Leader* and copied in "Mail Proposal," *Indianapolis News* (Feb. 16, 1968).

The annual reports of the Postmaster General for 1840, 1841 (an especially useful year), 1843, 1845, and 1883 are the best evidence of the alarm with which the Department viewed competition. In this connection, also see a letter of Mar. 30, 1844, from the Postmaster to Congress in answer to an inquiry about what was being done to suppress the carriers, printed as #213 in *Executive Documents* (28th Congress, 1st Session, 1843–44). Congressional debates leading to the passage of stricter laws may be found in the 1845 *Congressional Globe*. Public distaste for high government rates is evidenced by Joshua Levitt, *Cheap Postage* (Boston, 1848). Levitt is the source of the count of the 240 private expresses that at one time ran out of Boston; he also gives quotations from the *Report of the House Committee on the Post Office and Post Roads* (May 15, 1844) and one of several estimates that private carriers had half the mail business. The mail side of the express business is entertainingly sketched in "An American Enterprise,"

*Harpers New Monthly Magazine* (August 1875), which contains the cut of a carrier chased by government agents described in the text.

Of the many court cases, *United States* v. *Kochersperger* (Fed. Cas. 15,541, 1860) contains a detailed legislative history of the monopoly, *United States* v. *Easson* (18 Fed. 590, 1883) spelled the demise of the New York City messenger companies, and *United States* v. *Gray* (Fed. Cas. 15,253, 1840) exemplified jury hostility to the monopoly.


*Chapter Two*

The recent vintage of IPSA means that almost all the information about it comes from newspapers and periodicals: "Private Postmen Proliferate. . .," *Wall Street Journal* (Aug. 1, 1968); "Business Plays Post Office," *Business Week* (Aug. 17, 1968); "Private Post Office Plans Outlets Here," *New York Times* (June 7, 1969); "Money in Mail," *Newsweek* (Mar. 3, 1969); "Challenging Uncle Sam," *Newsweek* (Feb. 5, 1968); "Free Enterprise Mail Service Finds Success," *Colorado Springs Gazette Telegraph* (May 14, 1968); "Private Postal Service is Expanding," *New York Times* (Feb. 15, 1969); "Profits From Junk," *Colorado Springs Gazette Telegraph* (Aug. 29, 1968). There is also a series of articles by John G. Ackelmire in the *Indianapolis Star* (July 30–Aug. 2, 1968).

The other private services are reported in "The Stamp of Private Enterprise," *Wall Street Journal* (July 25, 1968); Leonard Sloane, "Companies Glad to Pay for Own Postal Service," *New York Times* (July 21, 1968); Scott R. Schmedel, "How Mel Skolnik, 28, Built an Empire. . .," *Wall Street Journal* (Aug. 27, 1969). "Playing Post Office," *Wall Street Journal* (June 5, 1967), tells what happens to companies that hire private carriers. The National Federation of Independent Business report on United Parcel is summarized in "Enterprise Beats Government," *Indianapolis Star* (Aug. 5, 1968).

Examples of the Post Office Department's embarrassing deficiencies have been culled from a variety of sources: Robert Sherrill, "Bring Back the Pony Express," *New York Times Magazine* (Nov. 3, 1968); Jack Harrison Pollack, "Can the Post Office Ever Be Efficient?" *Parade* (Aug. 25, 1968); "Taking Mail Out of Politics," *Time* (June 6, 1969); Philip Wagner, "It's Time Business Ran the Post Office," *Indianapolis Star* (April 27, 1968). Light is thrown on the Chicago debacle by a *New York Times* story (Apr. 9, 1967).

Fortunately there is a thorough and scholarly consideration of the legal aspects of the monopoly in Joseph F. Johnston, Jr., "The United States Postal Monopoly," *The Business Lawyer* (January, 1968).

The telegramletter concept is reported in "Post Office Studying Telegramletter Plan With Western Union," *Wall Street Journal* (March 28, 1969), and Roger W. Benedict, "Western Union Chief Strives to Maintain Wire Service While Building New Systems," *Wall Street Journal* (June 30, 1969).

The text indicates the importance of *Towards Postal Excellence: The Report of the President's Commission on Postal Organization* (Washington, 1968); it can be obtained for $1.25 from the Superintendent of Documents, Government Printing Office, Washington, D. C. 20402. Its genesis is described in "Your Letters May Be Stamped: 'U.S. Inc.,'" *New York Times* (July 21, 1968), and its result in "Administration to Ask Post Office Unit Be Converted into Government Corporation," *Wall Street Journal* (May 22, 1969). For union opposition to the idea see Willard Clopton, Jr., "Day Mourns 'ABCD' Mail Service End," *Washington Post* (Aug. 14, 1969). "Post Office Will Delay 75% of Building Awards," *Wall Street Journal* (Sept. 10, 1969), reenforces the Commission's contentions.

The encounter of the Post Office with the Louisiana Lottery is mentioned in Thomas Beer, *The Mauve Decade* (Vintage, 1951). There is a whole separate literature on postal censorship; used here were Robert W. Haney, *Comstockery in America* (Boston, 1960); James C. N. Paul and Murray L. Schwartz, *Federal Censorship: Obscenity in the Mail* (Free Press of Glencoe, 1961); and Zechariah Chafee, Jr., *Government and Mass Communications*, Vol. 1 (University of Chicago Press, 1947).


*Chapter Three*

All the material on Alaskan coins is extracted from Maurice M. Gould, Kenneth Bressett, Kaye and Nancy Detheridge, *Alaska's Coinage Through the Years* (Racine, Wisc., 1965).

The colonial tokens of Higley, Chalmers, Getz, and others are catalogued by Sylvester S. Crosby, *The Early Coins of America* (Boston, 1875). For Bechtler, Clarence Griffin, *The Bechtlers and Bechtler Coinage (Forest City Courier,* 1929), is indispensable. Lyman H. Low, *Hard Times Tokens* (New York, 1899), is the leading authority on the issues of the 1830's. Neil Carothers, *Fractional Money* (New York, 1930), discusses hard-times issues, while R. P. Falkner, "The Private Issue of Token Coins," *Political Science Quarterly,* treats both the Jackson and the Civil War tokens. For the individual varieties described in the text, reference must be made to George Hetrich and Julius Guttag, *Civil War Tokens and Tradesmen's Store Cards.* More detail on the Dix issues can be found in David C. Wismer, *Varieties of*

*Dix Civil War Tokens of the Year 1863* (Pennsylvania, 1922). Numismatic studies have provided color as well as facts; a writer in the *Coin Collector's Journal* (Vol. 1, p.12) is the source of the quotation eulogizing the Civil War tokens, while Charles I. Bushnell, *An Historical Account of the First Three Business Tokens Issued in the City of New York* (New York, 1859), supplied the rhapsody on tokens lost in attics.

Private depression issues are treated by Arthur Holch, "When Rubber Checks Didn't Bounce," *American Heritage* (June 1961). The most recent rash of token money is noted by William F. Rickenbacker, *Wooden Nickels* (Arlington House, 1966). The bridge case is *United States* v. *Monongahela River Bridge Co.* (Fed. Cas. 15,796, 1863); the amusement park token case is *United States* v. *Gellman* (44 F. Supp. 360).

*Chapter Four*

Any discussion of black private schools is initially indebted to Christopher Jencks, "Private Schools for Black Children," *New York Times Magazine* (Nov. 3, 1968); he suggests many of this chapter's themes and provides some of its illustrative details. A different view comes from Fred M. Hechinger, "Private Schools for the Slum Child?" *New York Times* (Dec. 29, 1968, Sec. IV, p. 11), but he agrees on the failures of the public schools and his statistics are used on that point. The retrospectively unrealistic solution of the Bundy Committee is outlined in Leonard Buder, "Bundy Panel Asks Community Rule for City Schools," *New York Times* (Nov. 8, 1967, p. 1).

Useful in the historical background section were R. Freeman Butts, *A Cultural History of Education* (New York, 1955), and William Cook Dunlap's published Ph.D. dissertation, *Quaker Education in Baltimore and Virginia* (University of Pennsylvania, 1933).

For the storefronts, the most comprehensive treatment is Joseph Featherstone, "Storefront Schools in Harlem," *New Republic* (Sept. 7, 1968). There are also a series of news stories in the *New York Times:* "IBM to Aid Harlem Youths" (Feb. 14, 1968, p. 45); "$767,800 Granted to Aid Police Here" (May 13, 1968, p. 38); "$200,000 Granted to Urban League" (Sept. 24, 1968, p. 41); "Football Aids Urban League" (Feb. 7, 1969, p. 40).

Harlem Prep has primarily attracted the attention of journalists: "I Can Do Anything," *Newsweek* (July 8, 1968); and in the *New York Times:* "Urban League Plans Harlem Prep School" (May 17, 1967, p. 1); Maurice Carroll, "Harlem Dropouts Head for College" (Oct. 3, 1967, p. 36); Bernard L. Collier, "A Dropout Picks Up Some Logic on His Way to College" (Mar. 14, 1968, p. 45); Homer Bigart, "Harlem Prep Gives

Dropouts a Door to College" (May 8, 1968, p. 49); "27 Dropouts Get Diplomas and Will Enter College" (June 18, 1968, p. 30); M. S. Handler, "Harlem Prep Graduates Told to Learn Not Rebel" (June 12, 1969, p. 1).

It is impossible to say how many other similar schools exist across the country. Those mentioned in the text were almost accidentally discovered through the following sources: Deidre Carmody, "L.I.U. to Help CORE Buy Its Pharmacy College," *New York Times* (July 11, 1968, p. 42); Steven V. Roberts, "Negroes Get Help at Church School," *New York Times* (May 7, 1967, p. 133); Peter Schrag, "Learning in a Storefront," *Saturday Review* (June 15, 1968); "Where Failures Make the Grade: Two Schools for Dropouts," *Carnegie Quarterly* (XVI, No. 4, Fall 1968); "A Private School to Open in Ghetto," *New York Times* (Aug. 28, 1966, p. 48); Lisa Hammel, "We Owe the Children a Lot More Than What They're Getting," *New York Times* (Apr. 19, 1968, p. 52); M. A. Farber, "Ford Fund Aids State-Backed Private School System in Boston," *New York Times* (Sept. 4, 1968, p. 28).

Public assistance for private schools was not too long ago considered wrong or visionary. Now it is making progress on both the legal and the political fronts, according to "Campus Communique," *Time* (Dec. 19, 1969). Russell Kirk described the California proposal in "From the Academy," *National Review* (June 17, 1969). The popular support accorded the private school is documented in Fred M. Hechinger, "Private Schools Win Favor in Poll," *New York Times* (June 29, 1969, p. 1).

The impact of the private schools is being felt in various ways. See David E. Rosenbaum, "A Capital Success Story," *New York Times* (Jan. 9, 1969, p. 68); Leonard Buder, "UFT Will Seek $18,000 Maximum," *New York Times* (Feb. 26, 1969, p. 1); "More Effective Schools Seek Larger Staff," *New York Times* (Jan. 19, 1969, p. 60); and Donald A. Erickson's essay in *Saturday Review* (Sept. 21, 1968).


*Chapter Five*

The medieval Fair Court cases are reported in volume 1 of the Selden Society's *Select Cases Concerning the Law Merchant* (London, 1908). The volume's introduction provides background information about the system, and other details come from the introduction of Philip Warren Thayer's *Cases and Materials on the Law Merchant* (Cambridge, 1939); F. D. MacKinnon, "Origins of Commercial Law," 52 *Law Quarterly Review* 30 (1936); Gilbert Langland, "The Origins of the Law of Sales," 29 and 31 *Law Quarterly Review* 442 and 50 (1913, 1915); Wyndham A. Bewes, *Romance of the Law Merchant* (London,

1923); and Julius H. Cohen, *Commercial Arbitration and the Law* (New York, 1918).

*Scott* v. *Avery,* with Lord Campbell's aspersion on fee-seeking judges, is in 25 *Law Journal,* page 313.

The nineteenth-century English background of arbitration and its development in the United States is recounted by Clarence F. Birdseye, *Arbitration and Business Ethics* (New York, 1926). Samuel Rosenbaum noted the 1883 letter to the *Times* in *A Report on Commercial Arbitration* (American Judicature Society, October 1916).

Wesley A. Sturges, "Commercial Arbitration or Court Application of Common Rules of Marketing," 34 *Yale Law Journal* 480 (1925), exemplifies the generally favorable treatment arbitration received from scholars in the twenties. But a new skepticism is apparent in "Rules of Law in Arbitration," 47 *Harvard Law Review* 590 (1934).

The modern debate, springing from Henrich Kronstein, "Arbitration is Power," 38 *New York University Law Review* 661 (1963), and the same author's earlier "Business Arbitration—Instrument of Private Government," 54 *Yale Law Journal* 36 (1944), is carried forward by Daniel G. Collins, "Commercial Arbitration and the UCC," 41 *New York University Law Review* 736 (1966); Charles Bunn, "Freedom of Contract Under the UCC," 2 *Boston College Industrial and Commercial Law Review* 59 (1960); Soia Mentschikoff, "Commercial Arbitration," 61 *Columbia Law Review* 846 (1961); E. J. Cohn, "Commercial Arbitration and the Rule of Law," 4 *University of Toronto Law Journal* 1 (1940); and Robert D. Crane, "Arbitral Freedom From Substantive Law," 14 *Arbitration Journal* 163 (1959).

Activities and procedures of the American Arbitration Association are outlined in its pamphlet, *Settling Private Disputes in the Public Interest* (n.p.n.d.). For modern applications, see Robert Coulson, "The Broadening Use of Arbitration," 24 *New York County Lawyers Association Bar Bulletin,* No. 1, (1966–67), p. 14.

*Chapter Six*

Statistics on public and private expenditures on crime prevention are compiled in *The Challenge of Crime in a Free Society* (1969), the report of the President's Commission on Law Enforcement and the Administration of Justice.

The introductory anecdote is from "Harlem Block Hires a Private Detective to Halt Burglaries," *New York Times* (Feb. 7, 1966). But the *Wall Street Journal* seems to have taken the most interest in voluntary policing activities: Alan M. Adelson, "Living With Fear: How Crime Terrorizes a Once-Peaceful Block in New York's Bronx" (Nov.

7, 1969); Norman Sklarewitz, "Vigilante Organizations Stir Increasing Concern Among Local Officials" (Oct. 9, 1969); David Gimpert, "Militant Jewish Group Sparks a Controversy in New York City Area" (Nov. 4, 1969); Pam Hollie, "Professional Thieves and Joy-Riding Kids Plague Boat Owners" (Aug. 29, 1969).

For the Black Panthers' origin as a patrol group, see Jerome H. Skolnick, *The Politics of Protest* (Ballantine, 1969); other information about the organization comes from S. Stern's article for the *New York Times Magazine* (Aug. 6, 1967).

The importance of Jeremiah P. Shalloo's *Private Police* (Philadelphia, 1933) is emphasized in the text. Henry Fielding as a police chief receives the attention of Patrick Pringle in *Henry and Sir John Fielding: The Thief Catchers* (London, 1968).

Charles Services activities were debated in *People* v. *Robinson,* 74 N.W.2d 41 (1955); the case received attention in a student note in 54 *Michigan Law Review* 1016 (1956). A phone call revealed that the company no longer operated in the police area.

All the material on Rural/Metropolitan Fire Protection Company is extracted from an unpublished speech by Lou Witzeman, "The Challenges Facing the Fire Service," delivered to the fall conference of the National Fire Protection Association on November 19, 1969, in Denver, Colorado.


*Chapter Seven*

For turnpike history, primary reliance was placed on John Austin Durrenberger, *Turnpikes: A Study of the Toll Road Movement in the Middle Atlantic States and Maryland* (Connecticut, 1968). It was the source of the Clay quotation used for a theme.

A great deal of unorganized information about the Valley Pike may be gleaned from John W. Wayland, *The Valley Turnpike—Winchester to Staunton* (1967). See also C. G. Wilkins, "Shenandoah Valley Turnpike Sold by Byrd 50 Years Ago," *Washington Post* (Jan. 1, 1970).

The Missouri committee discussions are reproduced verbatim in *Turnpikes and Toll Roads: Report of the Joint Turnpike Committee, Transcript of Proceedings of the Joint Turnpike Committee: Transcript of Testimony Before the Senate Committee* (Missouri General Assembly, 1953).

Wilfred Owen and Charles L. Dearing, *Toll Roads and the Problem of Highway Modification* (Brookings Institute, 1951), discuss postwar turnpikes.

The British economist quoted in the text is Gabriel J. Roth, author of *A Self-Financing Road System* (London, 1966).

*Chapter Eight*

Henrich Kronstein's 1944 article, cited for Chapter Five, expressed the fear that arbitration might work for private gain, not the public interest.

The best source for day-to-day operating details of the railroads during World War I is the trade magazine, *Railway Age.* The following issues were used: Feb. 8, 1918 (need for immediate car orders); Sept. 13, 1918 (delivery of first standardized cars); Dec. 20, 1918 (difficulties of standardization); June 6, 1919 (standardized wages); Dec. 5, 1919, issued Dec. 15, 1919 (up-from-the-bottom reforms); Jan. 24, 1919 (advertising, long hauling); and Dec. 13, 1918 (off-line freight agents).

Walker D. Hines wrote a *War History of American Railroads* (New Haven, 1928), which gives USRA's position. An almost contemporary analysis is William J. Cunningham, "The Railroads Under Government Operation," *Quarterly Journal of Economics* (1921); and Frank Haigh Dixon, *Railroads and Government* (New York, 1922), also treats the wartime nationalization. Surprisingly, there are important details about George N. Peek in Rixey Smith and Norman Beasley, *Carter Glass* (New York, 1939).

For other contemporary comment directly drawn on here, see Theodore H. Price, "The Government as Railway Manager," *Outlook* (Sept. 4, 1918); Walter Weyl, "The Railroad Administration to Date," *New Republic* (Nov. 9, 1918); and George N. Peek, "Speech Before U.S. Chamber of Commerce at St. Louis, April 29 [1919]," vertical file 16000, Library of Bureau of Railway Economics, Washington, D.C.

Paul Goodman's remark about centralization is from *People or Personnel* (Random House, 1963).

WILLIAM C. WOOLDRIDGE attended Harvard College with a National Merit scholarship, graduating *magna cum laude* in American history. He won a Richard Weaver fellowship for a year's study of medieval history at St. Andrews University in Scotland, then entered the University of Virginia School of Law, graduating in 1969. Along the way he published the *Harvard Conservative* for three years, did a stint on the *Virginia Law Review,* and had articles appearing in *National Review,* the *Virginia Magazine of History and Biography, Rally,* and *Intercollegiate Review.* He is now an Army lawyer, stationed in Heidelberg, Germany. After returning from his military service, he plans to practice in the area of administrative and corporate law. He is a member of the Virginia Bar, the American Bar Association, the Raven Society, and the Order of the Coif. He and his wife, the former Joyce Norton of Danville, Virginia, have a son, William Charles Wooldridge, Jr. *Uncle Sam, the Monopoly Man* is his first book.

44453